SCRAPPY WONKY
Quilt Block Extravaganza

12 Blocks · 13 Projects · Deceptively Simple & Fun

Shannon Roudhán and Jason Bowlsby

stashBOOKS.
an imprint of C&T Publishing

PUBLISHER Amy Barrett-Daffin	**PRODUCTION COORDINATOR** Tim Manibusan
CREATIVE DIRECTOR Gailen Runge	**ILLUSTRATOR** Aliza Shalit
SENIOR EDITOR Roxane Cerda	**PHOTOGRAPHY COORDINATOR** Rachel Ackley
TECHNICAL EDITOR Debbie Rodgers	**FRONT COVER PHOTOGRAPHY** by Jason Bowlsby
COVER/BOOK DESIGNER April Mostek	**PHOTOGRAPHY** by Jason Bowlsby, unless otherwise noted

Published by Stash Books, an imprint of C&T Publishing, Inc., P.O. Box 1456, Lafayette, CA 94549

Library of Congress Cataloging-in-Publication Data
Names: Roudhán, Shannon Leigh, 1967- author. | Bowlsby, Jason, 1970- author.
Title: Scrappy wonky quilt block extravaganza : 12 blocks, 13 projects, deceptively simple & fun / Shannon Roudhán and Jason Bowlsby.
Description: Lafayette, CA : Stash Books, an imprint of C&T Publishing, [2024] | Summary: "Make something FAB out of (seemingly) nothing at all! There are twelve blocks and thirteen accessible and beginner-friendly projects included inside for all quilters. Readers will learn how to use scraps, odd cuts, and small fabric treasures in unexpected ways to create one-of-a-kind quilts"-- Provided by publisher.
Identifiers: LCCN 2024004716 | ISBN 9781644034002 (trade paperback) | ISBN 9781644034019 (ebook)
Subjects: LCSH: Patchwork quilts. | Quilting--Patterns. | Patchwork--Patterns.
Classification: LCC TT835 .R6767 2024 | DDC 746.46--dc23/eng/20240310
LC record available at https://lccn.loc.gov/2024004716

Printed in China

10 9 8 7 6 5 4 3 2 1

ACKNOWLEDGMENTS AND DEDICATION

We are extremely grateful to, and would like to acknowledge, the following companies for their generous contribution of products to the making of this book.

- Aurifil Thread
- BERNINA of America, Inc.
- Cherrywood Hand Dyed Fabrics
- Clover USA
- C&T Publishing
- Hobbs Batting
- Reliable Corporation
- Robert Kaufman Fabrics

Special shout-out to Linda for being the voice in our corner ... watch out for the bears.

This book is dedicated to anyone who ever wanted to embrace their creative chaos but needed a little push. This is it ... this is your little push. STITCH ON!!

CONTENTS

THE BLOCKS   40

GOOD NEIGHBORS   40

ALL-SEEING EYE   43

LOVE SHACK   45

STEPPIN' UP   47

DOWN ON THE CORNER   49

ENTWINED   51

FLY AWAY HOME   55

DRUNKEN PINEAPPLE   57

SCRAPPY WONKY ROSE   59

DON QUIXOTE   62

WONKY NINE-PATCH   64

OH, MY STARS!   66

THE PROJECTS 88

The Method 89

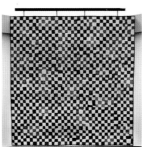

INTRODUCTION
A Word (or two) from Shannon & Jason

GETTING SCRAPPY

We both grew up with scrappy quilts made of leftover fabrics from clothing projects, garments that were past the point of repair, and even other quilts. Nobody ever really called them "scrappy quilts" because buying new fabric wasn't always an option, and reusing fabric was just how quilts were made. Even if purchased fabric was used, there was a good chance that someone's old housedress or remnants of those matching shirts someone made for you and your sibling that you couldn't wear without suffering the greatest of embarrassments to ever be heaped upon the head of any preteen ... ahem ... would show up as well.

Several years ago, we were inspired to dive back into scrappy quilting and improv piecing while doing research for our book *Boro & Sashiko, Harmonious Imperfection*. While researching that book, we came across the Japanese idiom of the three beans: A piece of fabric that is large enough to wrap three beans in is large enough to keep. That's a pretty small piece of fabric! We had always kept larger scraps and old clothing, but this concept of the three beans really challenged our notions of sustainability. So, in true "if it's good enough to be done, it's good enough to be overdone" fashion, we began putting the three-bean concept to the test and saved *all* of our scraps. In addition to our regular odd cuts, we started saving scraps that were the size of a single bean (never mind something that could wrap around three!) as well as threads and bits we called "dust." Well … now what to do with them? Make stuff! So, we sat down at our machines and started piecing together improv fabric, just to see how far those scraps could go. Random scraps turned into larger panels, until what was intended to be a simple wall hanging became what we affectionately call *The Beast*.

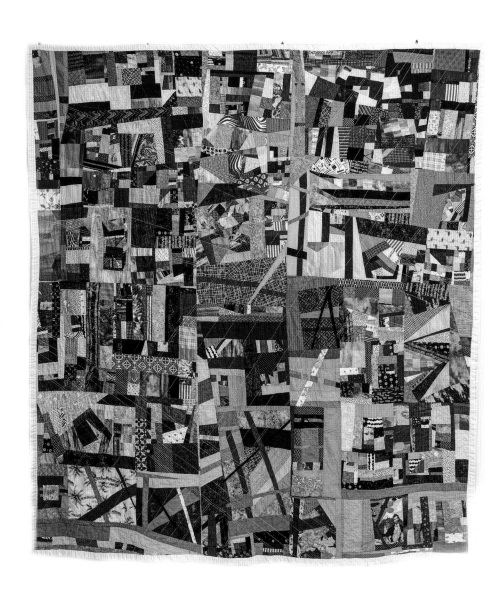

Quite by accident, while playing with piecing from a center starting point, we created what reminded us of a very not-up-to-code Log Cabin block. So, naturally, we made a few equally scrappy and wonky Log Cabin blocks on purpose. Although those Log Cabins never would have withstood the forces of nature, the scrappy fabric and randomly wonky nature of the blocks cast a spell on us that hasn't been broken to this day.

As we worked with these scrappy little structures and learned about the historical aspects of quilting and block building, a pattern emerged in our minds, and we began connecting the concept of harmonious imperfection from our previous book to these scrappy wonky quilt blocks. The imperfect perfection of scrappy wonky quilting quickly became an obsession that turned into our *Place* quilt and *The Colors of My Pride* quilt for LGBTQIA2S+ Pride Month here in the United States.

WHAT ARE SCRAPPY WONKY QUILT BLOCKS?

The process begins with visualizing a traditional quilt block. Hold that image in your mind. Then, re-create that quilt block without templates, precut pieces, or real concern about perfection, matching corners, and straight lines—just create based on what is seen. The end goal is to create a one-of-a-kind version of the original quilt block. There is no preplanned end game other than creating an amazing piece. For us, scrappy wonky style feels more organic than completely structured and planned. We hold the thought of what we are building in our mind or look at a reference piece, but the construction is not governed by strict rules.

That being said ... scrappy wonky quilt block construction does not simply mean slapping together pieces of fabric. As with any other quilt block construction, some preplanning and thoughtfulness in the process are needed to ensure that your blocks look wonky, not like a hot mess. Although blocks like Love Shack (page 45), Down on the Corner (page 49), and even the Scrappy Wonky Rose (page 59) can be created with a more free-flowing process and not much preplanning, we still break out the rulers and square templates when needed to ensure that we are going to end up with blocks that will fit a specific quilt or project. With blocks like Oh, My Stars! (page 66) and Drunken Pineapple (page 57), we reach for the ruler every step of the way to square up before moving on to the next step. If not, "wonky" quickly becomes "sloppy," and creative chaos turns into a general mess. As with all quiltmaking, good sewing and pressing techniques ensure that the blocks, although wonky, look beautiful in the finished pieces.

DIRECTED PLAY

With scrappy wonky quilting, you make your version of classic quilt blocks without the constraints of templates or pattern pieces. We do provide shapes, finished measurements, and an order of operation, but you won't find any templates because the blocks are completely wonky, with no preset measurements or exact pieces to precut. Some blocks have initial set measurements for cutting certain components, but then the wonky happens. So, stand tall and say out loud in your biggest Liam Neeson voice: "Release the WONK!"

FINAL THOUGHTS

The great thing about scrappy wonky quilt blocks is that if the mood strikes us or a color palette inspires us, we can sit down and make blocks—or even an entire project—right now. No looking for the templates or spending hours and hours on cutting. We just grab the colors that we love, and we're off!

If you have never made a quilt before, or if you are newer to quilting, you are going to love how forgiving this method of construction is. No ... really ... time after time, folx in our scrappy wonky quilt classes who were intimidated by matching corners and sewing perfect lines have been thrilled with how they can sit down and, with a basic machine that sews a straight line, create something glorious and stunning. Experienced quilters tell us that they love this style of construction because of the freedom of expression it offers and the modern aesthetic it creates. Most experienced quiltmakers love the sense of play in the creation of these blocks. The resulting randomness is always a thrill, whether you're new or experienced!

"Why would anyone want to take a big piece of fabric, cut it up into little pieces of fabric, and then sew those little pieces back together into a big piece of fabric?" – Jason's mom

She's not wrong ...

A VERY GOOD PLACE TO START

TOOLS

From the necessary to the why-do-we-have-that-thing, from the commonly known to the what-in-the-heck-is-that, we do love our gadgets. Here are the tools and gadgets we kept close at hand when creating the blocks and projects in this book.

Cutting Tools

Thread, fabric, batting, and interfacing—they all go to pieces with the proper cutting tools.

Small scissors that double as thread snips and for trimming on the fly. *Fig. A*

Thread snips for trimming away those little wisps. *Fig. B*

Large fabric scissors for those big jobs. Seriously ... don't let me catch you using my fabric shears to open that package! *Fig. C*

A rotary cutter with extra blades. Keep these sharp by replacing the blade as soon as you see a skip, and your fabric edges will be clean and crisp. A sharp rotary cutter blade cuts your work time in half. (See what we did there?) *Fig. D*

A.

B.

C.

D.

Quilting Rulers

Yes, we use some rulers in this book! Even in scrappy wonky piecing, we still need to square things up from time to time so the pieces fit together nicely.

Square and straight-edged quilting rulers are a must for squaring up wobbly cuts and uneven seams as well as trimming blocks to the correct size. Keep a good selection on hand. *Fig. A*

Cutting Mats

Cutting mats protect your surfaces, sure, but lined mats are vital for making quick mat cuts, too. We have an entire cutting table, but we have smaller cutting mats on side tables, on project tables, and at all of our sewing stations for quick adjustments and on-the-fly cutting. *Fig. B*

Rotating cutting mats are one of those tools we didn't realize we needed until we had one. They are unbelievably convenient for squaring up blocks without picking them up and repositioning them. Just give 'em a spin and cut! *Fig. C*

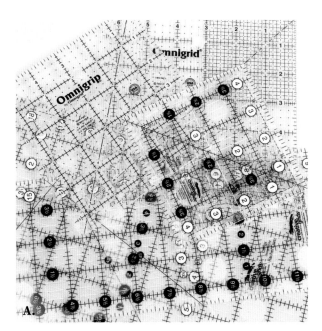

A.

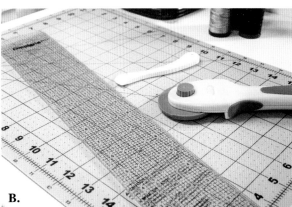

B.

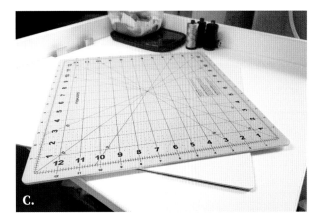

C.

Bent-Tip Tweezers

Bent-tip tweezers are typically used for threading a serger. We repurpose ours as a tool for coaxing small scraps of fabric through the machine evenly. *Fig. A*

A.

Seam Ripper

We all make mistakes or decide that a certain piece of fabric just wasn't supposed to go there. Seam ripper to the rescue! Pro tip: Keep a few of these around … that way *someone* isn't always walking in and *stealing* yours … just sayin'. *Fig. B*

B.

Machine Needles

Machine needles come in types and sizes for every imaginable sewing project, and we have most of them in our sewing cabinet drawers. For our projects in this book, we mainly used SCHMETZ Universal Needles size 70/10. Universal needles and quilting needles work great as well, and we keep a supply of jeans needles close at hand for those heavier fabrics and weightier threads. We buy ours in boxes of 100 because we are strict about changing our needles after every eight hours of sewing—and so should you. This habit ensures that the needles are always sharp and can pierce the fabric without tearing or popping threads. *Fig. C*

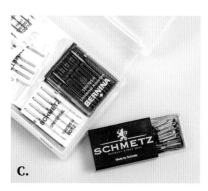

C.

Hand-Sewing Needles

If you are a hand sewist, you can absolutely do hand piecing on some of or all the projects in this book. We are both hand sewists and use Clover Black Gold Appliqué/Sharps in a variety of sizes, depending on the fabric we are working with. *Fig. D*

D.

Hand-Quilting Needles

Speaking of hand quilting, if you are interested in trying your hand (see what we did there?) at this skill, grab an assortment pack and see which size works best for you. We use the Clover Black Gold Quilting Between needles in a variety of sizes, depending on the density of the fabric and the thickness of the sandwich. For "big-stitch quilting," we like to use sashiko needles. Which brings us to … *Fig. E*

E.

Sashiko Needle and Thimble

Most of our hand quilting is inspired by the sashiko patterns and techniques in our book *Boro & Sashiko, Harmonious Imperfection*. For those projects where we did sashiko quilting, we used sashiko needles and palm thimbles. *Fig. A*

Easy Threading Needles

This is another tool that we didn't know we needed until we tried it. Easy threading needles are invaluable for picking up quilting thread ends and burying them. The entire process takes far less time than threading the standard eye of a regular needle for each quilting thread end that needs to be buried. *Fig. B*

Thimble

Whether you are hand piecing, burying threads, or sewing rod pockets and borders, you're going to want a thimble to project those fingertips. If this is your first time hand sewing, there are quite a few thimbles to choose from, so pick the ones that work best for your hands. *Fig. C*

Pins

Quilting pins are an essential tool for piecing and assembling blocks. They keep the edges lined up as you sew and ensure that the seams match perfectly. We find that we always appreciate having a magnetic pin holder next to our machine. *Fig. D*

Clips

Fabric clips like Wonder Clips by Clover are the tool we most often use when assembling and binding quilts. It just takes a quick flip of the finger to pull them off as you sew—no stopping and starting needed. *Fig. E*

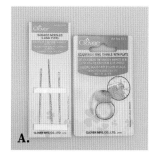

A.

B.

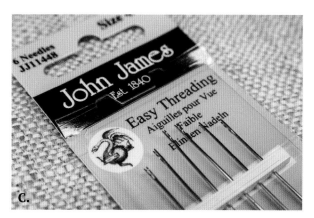

C.

D.

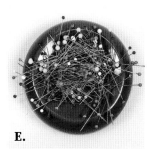

E.

F.

Marking Tools

Unless you are an expert free-motion quilter, you are going to have to draw lines on your fabric to follow for quilting. We use a variety of wash-away markers, heat-erasable pens, and, more often than not, the Hera Marker by Clover to score our favorite patterns before we sit down and start the business of quilting. Air-erasable markers or washable markers are a good choice for those small projects that you can finish in one sitting, but for projects that will take more time, choose a longer-wearing option. Our go-to for marking our projects are the White Marking Pen by Clover and a Hera Marker. Tools like the Hera Marker have a fine edge along one side that, with gentle pressure, can be used to crease or score fabric without leaving a permanent mark. Be sure to test any marking tool on a fabric scrap **before** you mark that quilt you spent weeks constructing! *Fig. A*

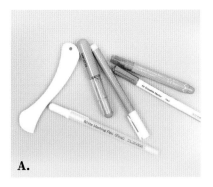

A.

Basting Tools

When it comes to sewing the sandwich of layers together—the quilting—we almost always opt for basting spray. This forgiving spray lightly adheres the layers together but allows for minor adjustments. Another option is coilless safety pins. They are inexpensive, but they can be more difficult to use for large quilt projects, as the layers can easily shift and skew as you sew. *Fig. B*

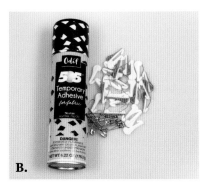

B.

Sewing Machine

Any sewing machine capable of a straight stitch and with a powerful-enough motor can handle all the piecing and quilting shown in this book. We used a BERNINA 570QE and our BERNINA 790 PLUS for the piecing and the quilting. *Fig. C*

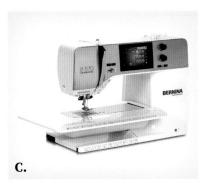

C.

Thread

We want to give a special mention here to thread—specifically, the way we list thread in the Materials section of the projects. For the general piecing of all blocks, we used a neutral color of Aurifil thread, chosen based on the overall color composition of the block being made. That said, most scrappy wonky blocks have lights and darks in them, so our go-to was Aurifil 50WT in blonde beige (#5010). This thread is not listed in the individual projects, but we do note when we used a different color or weight of Aurifil thread for quilting, assembling the quilt top, or binding. *Fig. D*

D.

CUTTING UP

Measurements

Throughout this book, you will find different types of measurements and, in case this is your first time going scrappy wonky, we thought it would be a good idea to familiarize you with some of our terminology.

Cut Measurements

Cut measurements are an exact set of numbers given for the specific measurements of a cut piece of fabric. Instructions for the dimensions of borders, sashing, and garment pieces are all given in exact measurements and should be cut accordingly.

Trimmed Measurements

Most of these blocks are created with edges that run well outside the needed dimensions for the project. For example, the Entwined (page 51) and Scrappy Wonky Rose (page 59) blocks have uneven edges that are then cut to size with a quilting square or ruler. That size is the trimmed measurement that the blocks and panels need to be to even up their edges so they fit in the finished project. The trimmed measurement is an exact measurement and should not be deviated from if you are making the project exactly as shown.

Finished Measurements

Finished measurements are the set of exact numbers assigned to a block or a project after the piece is assembled. For example, the finished measurement of a 10½″ × 10½″ (26.7 × 26.7cm) block is 10″ × 10″ (25.4 × 25.4cm) because a ¼″ (6mm) seam allowance is used on each side when the blocks are assembled. The finished measurements of a throw might be 65″ × 70″ (165 × 178cm), but the dimensions prior to adding the border or binding would be 65½″ × 70½″ (166 × 179cm).

Ish Measurements

Throughout this book, you will see what we call *ish* measurements. Ish measurements are not exact—they are close, but not precise. Think of them as more of a target range; as long as you are close to the ish measurement, you will be fine. This approach also means that other than finished measurements or unless otherwise stated, all measurements given should be assumed to be ish measurements. For example, for the blocks using strips, we might give you an ish measurement of 2-ish inches (5-ish cm) for the width of each strip. This direction means that you could use strips that are narrower, wider, or not the same width along the length of the strip, BUT they should be close-ish to 2-ish inches (5-ish cm) to achieve the same look as our finished blocks.

In some instances, we provide the ish measurements we used so you have a starting point. Folx usually find that having that starting point is enough to move the process forward for their first few blocks, and then they tend to go off on their own from there. And that's just fine by us ... encouraged even! Ish measurements are the true foundation of scrappy wonky quilt blocks.

Making the Cut

Something should be said here about the cuts made to achieve the best possible scrappy wonkiness. We break our cuts down into three categories: ruler cuts, mat cuts, and free cuts.

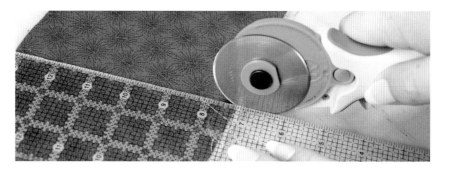

Ruler Cuts

Ruler cuts are precise cuts made with quilting rulers or other straight edges. These are essential for achieving the correct finished size of a project. Ruler cuts are also the place to start your scrappy wonky journey. For most of the blocks, you don't have to cut pieces to exact widths and lengths, but you do want clean cuts that don't wobble too much, or your seams will bunch and ripple. **Remember: Scrappy wonky doesn't mean sloppy!** So, use those rulers to keep your cuts clean and tidy to make your sewing and finishing easier.

Mat Cuts

Yes, we do use a mat for all of our cuts because we don't want our rotary cutters scarring up our tables. But *mat cuts* describes the process of using the lines on a mat as starting and ending point guides to make your cuts. To make a mat cut, lay your fabric on the mat and look for the first point of reference: a preprinted line on the mat, extending from one end of your fabric. Place your rotary cutter on this point. Then, find your second point of reference: the corresponding point of the same preprinted line as it emerges on the opposite side of your fabric. Keep your eye on that second point as you move your rotary cutter smoothly along the invisible line created by the two points. This technique takes a little practice, but once you become more skilled with making clean lines with mat cuts, you will find that you are able to be freer with your pieces, further enhancing the scrappy wonkiness of your blocks.

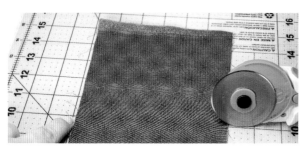

Free Cuts

Free cuts are the untethered joy of scrappy wonky blocks. Simply lay your fabric on your cutting surface, set the rotary cutter at the starting point, focus on the ending point of the cut, and cut along that invisible line—no rulers, no rules. These cuts are perfect for shorter strips and pieces for blocks like Love Shack (page 45) and Scrappy Wonky Rose (page 59), where precise measurements are not required and would even hinder the wonkiness of your finished blocks.

Don't be afraid to try out mat cuts and free cuts. If you have been using rulers for these types of cuts for a while, you are probably going to be able to make mat cuts and even free cuts fairly easily. And, as with all physical skills, the more you do it, the better you become!

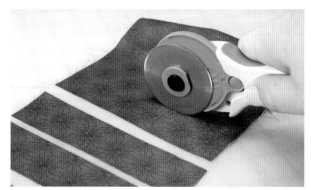

SEAMS SO RIGHT

We have said it before, and we will say it again: Scrappy wonky does not mean sloppy! Being mindful of neat, tidy seams is important to ensure that your scrappy wonky project isn't a buckled, warped mess. If you haven't done a lot of sewing before, it might take a little practice, but never fear! We have included blocks in this book, such as Good Neighbors and Love Shack, that allow you to practice sewing and still end up with stunning finished pieces.

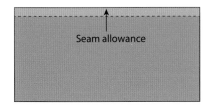

Seam allowance

The term *seam allowance* refers to the distance between the sewn line (the line of thread your machine makes) and the cut edge (or raw edge) of the fabric. For most of our piecing, we use a ¼″ (6mm) seam allowance, but sometimes we find it necessary to use a slightly narrower or wider seam allowance, depending on the piecing and the thickness of the fabric.

When the scraps we are sewing together are very small, we use a slightly narrower seam allowance. For example, in the starting pieces for the smallest of the Love Shack blocks (page 45), the scraps were often so tiny that we used a ⅛″ (3mm) seam allowance so the entire scrap wasn't eaten up in the seam allowance. We use this ⅛″ (3mm) seam allowance for any mini blocks made from tiny scraps, as long as the fabric is dense enough that the narrow seam allowance doesn't fray the edges and leave a hole in the final project. That's a heartbreak we want to help you avoid.

TIP • Stitch length

We like to use a 2.0mm stitch length (approximately 13 stitches per inch) for making our blocks. This length is shorter than the default most machines are set to, so be sure to check yours and reset as needed. This shorter stitch length ensures that your pieces will be secure, even with narrower seam allowances, like ⅛″ (3mm).

Due to the wonky nature of the construction of strip blocks and their assembly into larger blocks or projects, we often use a slightly wider seam allowance than ¼″ (6mm). When you join these strip-pieced blocks together, the differing width of the strips means that the joining seams will not line up nice and neat, which can cause the fabric to shift under the presser foot of your machine, resulting in a bit of havoc with your assembly—and a wonky sewn line is not the kind of wonky you want. The All-Seeing Eye block (page 43) is a prime example of a block where a generous ¼″ (6mm) seam allowance is necessary. The All-Seeing Eye block is a four-square block made up of strips of fabric of varying widths. When you sew the first two blocks together to create the four-square, the thicker fabric created by the multiple seams often requires a generous ¼″ (6mm) seam allowance to ensure that the seams from the

strips are secured properly rather than fighting against one another and skewing your sewn line, causing the assembled blocks to buckle and warp. Once the final four-square is being sewn together, we like to use a generous ¼″ (6mm) seam allowance again because we are sewing together two sets of these bulkier seams. Because we are using this generous ¼″ (6mm) seam allowance to assemble our blocks, we add a slightly wider seam allowance to our initial blocks when we are creating them and squaring them up.

TIP • Don't Get It Twisted

To prevent a beautiful seam from becoming a twisted disaster while you're sewing pieces or blocks together, place the seams from pieced fabric on top and flat or flatter fabric on the bottom (facing the feed dogs). This is not always possible, but when it is, layering them this way can prevent seam ripping and resewing to untwist a mangled seam.

We love using nontraditional quilting fabrics for our pieces, including denim, canvas, and heavier muslins. These fabrics are slightly thicker than quilting cotton, and sewing them with a ¼″ (6mm) seam allowance results in a seam that, once pressed, is more than ¼″ (6mm), sometimes by ⅛″ (3mm) or more. The folding over and pressing of these thicker fabrics actually takes a measurable amount of fabric and can result in your finished blocks being too small. Rather than sewing a narrower seam allowance, our preferred method when sewing heavy fabrics like denim is to cut our pieces larger and sew a ¼″ (6mm) seam allowance. How do we know which fabrics to do this with and how much wider to make our blocks? Practice. If a fabric feels thicker or denser than your quilting cottons, practice assembling a block with it to see how it works out. Yup … it's that simple. Cut up some scraps and sew them together in a simple construction like the Good Neighbors block (page 40) to get a feel for it. In the end, you will gain practice and have a finished piece that you can use for a future project, regardless of the trimmed size. *TA-DA!*

PRESSING MATTERS

Do not underestimate the power of a hot, heavy, steamy iron when making all of those tiny little scrappy wonky seams lay flat and even. Achieving the flattest, most even seams possible is important to prevent visible bumps in the finished fabric and vital to create even quilting lines. Those lumps and bumps will throw off even the thickest needle being driven by the best sewing machine and give

you uneven seams and jagged quilting lines. Mostly, a good, steamy iron will do the trick, but when even the power of pressing with an iron isn't enough, the combo of your steam iron and a good seam clapper or a rubber mallet will come in mighty handy. What's that? Are we advocating for whacking and pounding your seams flat? YUP! You bet your sweet bippy we are! Seam clappers have long been the friend of garment sewists to ensure that seams are as flat as possible before finishing. We have called our seam clapper into action for additional pressing *oomph* on our scrappy wonky and improv fabrics on numerous occasions. If you can't find one, you can make a quick trip to your local hardware

store for a rubber mallet (or maybe snag one from your neighbor's workbench). Then, steam and press your seams with your iron and *whack* them into shape. This combo is particularly useful when you have a dense section of scrappy seams meeting up in one spot (as in the Scrappy Wonky Rose, page 59), and they absolutely must be flattened out (again, that Scrappy Wonky Rose block). It might seem a bit unconventional, but don't be afraid to put some clap and whack power into your work for perfectly pressed seams that won't bog down your needle when you are adding another piece of fabric or quilting your creations. Wonky is good in our blocks ... not in our finishing.

Seam clapper

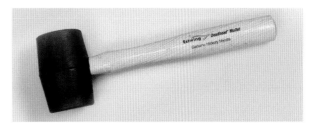

Rubber mallet

PRESSING VS. IRONING

Pressing = Applying steady pressure directly downward with an iron or pressing tool

Ironing = Moving the iron around, such as for smoothing out large pieces of fabric or garments

Pressing sets the thread on a seam, sets the seam itself, or sets the fabric squarely without moving the fabric around and stretching it out of shape. When you're pressing blocks made from separate pieces, they will press more squarely without having warped seams and joins.

Nesting

When you just have to have that perfect center when you are joining four finished blocks, nesting is how to make it happen. Nesting works beautifully for assembling a Four-Patch or when assembling the blocks for a project. For the block construction in this book, we strictly adhere to the wonky part of the scrappy wonky piecing and are less concerned about creating perfect angles and flawless points … until it comes to joining our blocks. For this process, we employ a technique that is so simple, it would be just silly to pass up: nesting.

1. Using four blocks sewn in sets of 2, make sure that the seams on each set are pressed in opposite directions (for instance, top set pressed to the left, bottom set to the right).

2. With right sides facing, hold the 2 sets of blocks together and line up the channel created by the sewn seams. *Fig. A*

3. Gently work the 2 channels together so one fits (nests) inside the other. *Fig. B*

4. Secure the nested seams by placing a clip over the spot or, for even more stability, securing both sides of the seam with 2 pins or a single u-pin. *Figs. C-E*

5. Sew the seam, open, press, and … presto! Your seams match perfectly. *Fig. F*

A.

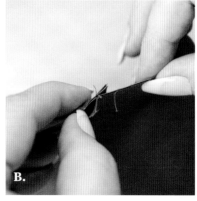

B.

C.

D.

E.

F.

Spinning Seams

"You spin me right 'round, baby" sticks in our heads every time we execute this technique. Every. Time. Spinning seams is not as much fun as dancing the night away in an '80s club, but it is pretty magical and produces an almost flawlessly flat center seam when four blocks are joined together.

1. Sew a set of 4 blocks together, using nesting (page 20).

2. Lay the assembled blocks face down on a pressing mat. *Fig. A*

3. Finger-press the seams so they are spinning in a pinwheel style away from one another. It helps to keep in mind that you are distributing the fabric evenly inside the joined seam, so you will press away from the thickest seams. *Fig. B*

4. Work into the center of the seam with a pressing tool to separate the layers in the direction of the rest of the pinwheel seam. Finger-press the seam open. Here, it creates a tiny checkerboard effect in the center of the seam. *Figs. C-D*

5. Press the seams flat with an iron, using the tip of the iron to press the center flat. *Fig. E*

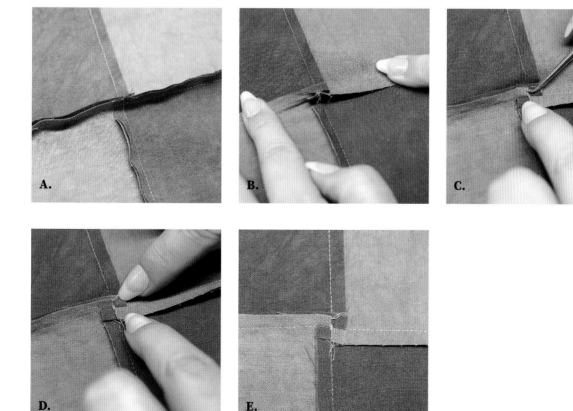

A.

B.

C.

D.

E.

Pressing and Sewing on the Bias

When cutting fabric, you cut either with the grain, across the grain, or on the bias.

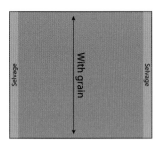

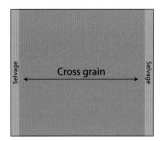

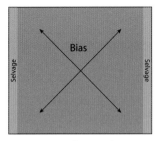

Cuts with the grain of the fabric are made parallel to the selvedge. Cuts with the grain have almost no stretch at all.

Cuts across the grain (or cross grain) of the fabric are made perpendicular to the selvedge. Cross-grain cuts have a little stretch.

Bias cuts are diagonal cuts and have a great deal of stretch.

This detail is not something you have to be overly cautious about on smaller scrap seams, but on longer bias cuts, such as for the Wonky Nine Patch (page 64) or the Don Quixote (page 62) blocks, and even on the small bias seams of the star blocks, you need to be mindful of sewing and pressing to prevent warps and stretching. Bias cuts are the stretchiest fabric cuts, so you must be careful to not move the iron and warp your seams when pressing. Additionally, don't pull on your fabric as it feeds into the presser foot on your machine, or it will stretch and cause a rippled seam, making your entire block buckle.

Often, the real challenge when working with cut scraps is that you don't know where that scrap came from or how it was cut—with the grain, cross grain, or bias. If you are concerned about larger scraps being sewn or pressed on the bias, do a gentle stretch test. Virtually no stretch is a cut with the grain, a small amount of stretch is cut across the grain, and a bias cut will easily stretch with the gentlest pull. Don't discard these scraps! Simply be mindful of how you handle them when pressing and sewing.

Into the Thick of It

When you're working with nontraditional quilting fabrics, such as denim, tapestry, and home decor fabrics, the sewn seams can very quickly become unmanageably thick. To prevent this issue, rather than pressing your seams outward, press them open. Doing so distributes the fabric more evenly and makes the final piece lay flatter.

TO WASH OR NOT TO WASH?

There is really no question here at all ... not for us. Every piece of fabric that comes into this house, whether from the brick-and-mortar fabric rescue, an online fabric rescue, a thrift shop, or a tag sale—yes, even charm packs and scrap bags—is washed and pressed as quickly as possible. This habit prevents introducing critters to our abode and removes most of the treatments (including pesticides) and sizing from the fabrics. If washing doesn't seem necessary or the scraps can't be washed, we bag 'em up and chuck 'em in the freezer for a day or so to kill off any fabric-munching critters that might be hitching a ride. Besides, it is *so* nice to do a fabric pull and dive right into a project without waiting for the wash and dry cycles and then having to lug out the iron and board. A little effort in the beginning makes it easier to embrace the creative chaos when it strikes!

THINGS YOU OUGHTA KNOW

Techniques

Hand Stitches

The ladder stitch and appliqué stitch are two essential skills we teach in all of our hand-sewing workshops. Here, we use them for hand-sewing binding, facing, rod pockets, and quilt labels.

Ladder Stitch: This stitch goes by "ladder stitch" or "slip stitch," depending upon who taught you. Both are correct ... just don't tell your Aunt Betty or Grandpa Lou we said so. We use the stitch to invisibly close folded seams, such as those in pillows, placemats, and coasters, as well as the *Star Stuff* wall hanging (page 106).

1. Bring the needle up from inside the fold in the seam allowance. This technique hides the knot inside the fold of the seam allowance.

2. Sewing through only the folded fabric of the seam allowance, make a small stitch on the fabric opposite the seam. Your needle should go into the fabric adjacent to where it just came out, behind the fold to hide the thread. The stitch should be no longer than ¼″ (6mm), or your finished seam will pucker.

3. Make a small stitch in the opposite side of the seam; again, your needle should go through the fabric directly across from where it just came out, traveling behind the fold no farther than ¼″ (6mm).

4. Repeat Steps 2 and 3, pulling on your thread every few inches to close up the seam. When you pull the thread, be careful not to pucker the seams.

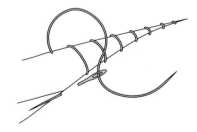

Appliqué Stitch: The appliqué stitch is a finishing stitch used to attach quilt labels, hanging rods, and the folded side of bindings. If correctly done, the edge of the folded fabric covers the stitches below, making the sewing invisible.

1. Secure your thread to the back side of your folded piece, bias, or hem.

2. Take a stitch into the main fabric, picking up only a thread or two.

3. Place the needle again to the back side of the folded hem/bias/facing near your last stitch and run it through the folded fabric just below the edge, moving no farther than ¼″ (6mm).

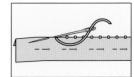

4. Again, take a thread or two of fabric from the main fabric adjacent to where your needle came out of the fold.

5. Continue in this manner, tightening up every few stitches.

Hong Kong Finish

If you are an accomplished garment sewist, you are probably already well acquainted with Hong Kong finishes for seams. This technique is our preferred method for reducing bulk in quilted garments and creates beautifully encased seams.

Although it is a little bit of extra work, the Hong Kong finish adds a touch of elegance and finesse to any unlined garment. Who knows, you may want to hang your jacket inside out just to show off your Hong Kong seam finish. What? Just us?

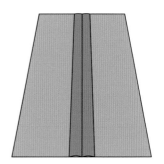

A.

1. Stitch the seam and press the seam allowances open. *Fig. A*

2. Attach the first side of the bias tape. Place the right side of the bias tape against one side of the seam and sew a ¼″ (6mm) seam. Watch carefully to avoid stretching the bias tape as you sew, as doing so will cause the seam edge warp. *Fig. B*

3. Press the seam open and then wrap the tape around the garment seam edge, bringing the remainder of the tape to the back and encasing seam edge. Press gently. *Fig. C*

4. Sew through the seam allowance and bias tape. *Fig. D*

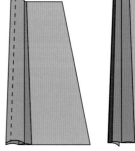

B.   C.

Folding the garment back out of the way so you are only sewing through the garment seam allowance, sew in the furrow next to the edge of the folded tape with an edge-stitch foot, following the seam you just made (aka "stitch in the ditch"). If done correctly, the stitches disappear into the ditch of the seam and are not visible on the front side of the seam.

You can also sew in this same method, but through the seam allowance **and** the garment body. This method gives a visible line of stitches on the front of the garment that we think looks pretty snazzy.

D.

5. Repeat Steps 2–4 for the second side of the seam. *Fig. E*

Finished Hong Kong seam

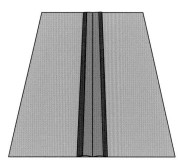

E.

TERMINOLOGY

Binding

Binding is a finishing step for a project where fabric is attached along the edges of the assembled quilt top or project and then attached again to the opposite side. It encases all the layers and protects the raw edges. A binding can be made wider or narrower to act as an accent border.

Border

A *border* is the fabric around the outside of an assembled quilt. The border can be one piece of fabric or assembled from multiple pieces of fabric.

Combo Block

A *combo block* is created when two or more blocks are framed together to make a single larger block. This is accomplished by creating two blocks that fit inside a larger single block and then filling in the empty space with filler fabric or background fabric. This is an evolved version of framing.

Component Block

Component blocks are smaller blocks that are sewn together to create a larger block called a compound block.

The four component blocks of the Four-Patch block

Compound Block

A *compound block* is a larger block made up of smaller blocks called component blocks. Four-Patch and Nine-Patch blocks are examples of compound blocks because they are made up of four and nine blocks, respectively.

The All-Seeing Eye (page 43) block is a compound block made up of four component blocks.

The Oh, My Stars! (page 66) block is a compound block made up of nine component blocks.

The Ditch

As in "stitch in the ditch," the *ditch* is the channel created by a sewn seam, as seen from the front of the project. It is important for reference when quilting and for assembling blocks for nesting.

Framing

Framing is the act of adding background fabric to surround a block or blocks, which serves mechanical and aesthetic purposes. Framing serves the mechanical purpose of allowing you to use a block in a project with other blocks of varying sizes, while preserving the scrappy wonky aesthetics of the individual blocks.

Facing

Facing is a kind of binding in that it holds the layers of the quilt together, but a facing does not show on the front of the quilt. It presents a clean edge that does not disrupt the design of the quilt top.

Facing does not show on the front side of the quilt, but it still wraps around and attaches to the back of the quilt.

Leftovers

No, this term doesn't refer to your Wednesday night dinner. *Leftovers* are the scraps and odd cuts that remain upon the completion of a previous project. Keep in mind that even these scrappy wonky blocks will create more leftovers, which can be used in other scrappy wonky blocks. And the circle of life continues.

Sashing

Sashing is fabric that runs between the blocks of a quilt.

Scraps

Scraps refer to those bits and pieces of fabric left over from previous projects as well as cast-offs, last season's *gasp* fat quarters and jelly rolls, odd cuts from flat-fold tables, end-of-the-bolt sales, thrift shops, tag sales, remnants, garage sales, your friend's fabric stash (because they weren't using that anyway, so why should it languish in a bin or on a shelf?), and any fabric previously purchased because you just had to have it but never did find the right project for it. All of these are fair game as scraps.

Seam Allowance

The *seam allowance* (sa) is the distance between the sewn line (the line of thread your machine makes) and the cut edge of the fabric.

Wonk It Up!

Once upon a time, we were teaching a virtual scrappy wonky workshop. Jason was watching the screen for questions and coaching students, while Shannon was sewing on the machine. One student asked

what to do if the blocks didn't look wonky enough, and Jason replied that they should just "Wonk it up!" The result was, apparently, a spontaneous virtual dance party with Jason and the students singing, "Wonk it up, wonk it up!" (Shannon had her back turned and did not see it at first but was alerted to the chaos by the giggles and hoots coming from the computer.)

Wonk it up! refers to placing or cutting a fabric piece so it is wonkier to increase the degree of wonk in the finished block. When in doubt … "wonk it up!"

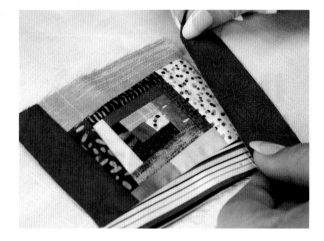

FOUR-PATCH AND NINE-PATCH BLOCKS

Four-Patch and Nine-Patch blocks are larger blocks, built by sewing together smaller blocks. Both can be created with straight cuts, wonky cuts, or a combination of the two.

A Four-Patch block is made by sewing together four smaller blocks.

A Nine-Patch block is made by sewing together nine smaller blocks.

Four-Patch and Nine-Patch blocks are compound blocks made up of smaller component blocks. Those component blocks can be made from solid pieces of fabric or comprise strips or pieces. Regardless of the types of cuts or materials used, the most important detail of all Four- and Nine-Patch blocks is that the component blocks measure up to the desired trim size of the larger block. To ensure that is the case, you must follow a few rules for Four- and Nine-Patch blocks to create blocks that fit the project correctly. We give you specific trimmed measurements for the blocks needed for each project, but in case you want to adapt a Four- or Nine-Patch to use for another project, here is an easy rule to follow:

Divide the total width of the finished block by the number of component blocks included, then add ½″ (1.2cm) seam allowance to each of those component blocks.

Four-Patch Calculations

For example, a Four-Patch block with a finished width of 10″ (25.4cm) is 2 blocks wide, so we divide the finished width by 2.

10″ (25.4cm) ÷ 2 blocks = 5″ (12.7cm)

5″ (12.7cm) + ½″ (1.2cm) seam allowance = 5½″ (14cm) component block

To make a 10″-wide (25.4cm) Four-Patch, you need 5½″ × 5½″ (14 × 14cm) blocks. Because a Four-Patch is constructed with 4 component blocks, you need 4 square component blocks that are each 5½″ × 5½″ (14 × 14cm).

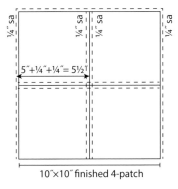

10″×10″ finished 4-patch

Nine-Patch Calculations

In this book, we include square and wonky-cut Nine-Patch blocks.

Square-Cut Nine-Patch

Square-cut Nine-Patch blocks, such as Oh, My Stars! (page 66), are created from individual pieces that are the same shape and size.

In the case of square-cut Nine-Patch blocks, the finished width is divided by 3. To cut three pieces of the same size, the finished width of the Nine-Patch component blocks needs to be divisible evenly by 3. For this reason, square-cut Nine-Patch blocks are made with finished widths of 3, 6, 9, 12, and so forth.

For example, a square-cut Nine-Patch block with a finished width of 9″ (23cm) is 3 blocks wide, so we divide the finished width by 3.

9″ (22.9cm) ÷ 3 blocks = 3″ (7.6cm)

3″ (7.6cm) + ½″ (1.2cm) seam allowance = 3½″ (8.9cm) component block

To make a 9″-wide (22.9cm) Nine-Patch, you need 3½″ × 3½″ (8.9 × 8.9cm) blocks. Because a Nine-Patch is constructed with 9 component blocks, you need 9 square component blocks that are each 3½″ × 3½″ (8.9 × 8.9cm).

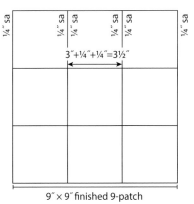

9″ × 9″ finished 9-patch

But what about the blocks for *The Full Monty* quilt (page 112)? Aren't those 10″ × 10″ (25.4 × 25.4cm) finished blocks? Why, yes, they are. And in the case of scrappy wonky blocks, we don't have to stick to all the rules. Making a 10″ × 10″ (25.4 × 25.4cm) finished nine-patch block by using traditional methods can be a measuring and cutting nightmare. Fortunately, using scrappy wonky piecing, to make a 10″ × 10″ (25.4 × 25.4cm) finished Oh, My Stars! block (page 66) for *The Full Monty* quilt, we made a 9″ × 9 (22.9 × 22.9cm) finished block and then framed it. (See Squaring Up and Framing, page 31.) Or, even better, you could make one- or two-star blocks and frame them together for a FAB multi-block! The choice is yours.

Wonky-Cut Nine-Patch: Stack, Slash, and Swap

Wonky-cut Nine-Patch blocks are created from a starting block and then cut into smaller individual pieces that are not the same shape or size.

The component blocks for the Wonky Nine-Patch are created by using a stack, slash, and swap method, so no exacting cuts are made for the nine component blocks that are needed. Just make a quick calculation to obtain the size of the starting block, and then you're on your way!

First, divide the total width of the finished block by the number of wonky pieces wide that the block is made from (in this case, 3). Then, add ½″ (1.2cm) seam allowance to each of those blocks. For a Scrappy Wonky Nine-Patch, that means adding 1½″ (3.8cm) to the width of the size of the finished block.

For example, to make a 10″ × 10″ (25.4 × 25.4cm) finished Wonky Nine-Patch block, start with two 11½″ × 11½″ (29.2 × 29.2cm) squares, stacked (10″ (25.4cm) + 1½″ (3.8cm)).

To make the 10″ × 10″ (25.4 × 25.4cm) finished Four-Patch version of the Wonky Nine-Patch block for *The Full Monty* quilt, start with 4 squares that are 6½″ × 6½″ (16.5 × 16.5cm), stacked in two different stacks.

Then, vertically slash those stacked squares. Swap the side pieces with the ones below, and then sew.

Repeat the process, slashing horizontally and swapping the tops and bottoms.

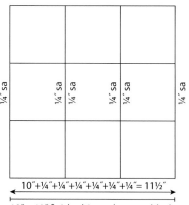

10″+¼″+¼″+¼″+¼″+¼″+¼″= 11½″

10″ × 10″ finished 9-patch starter block

SQUARING UP AND FRAMING

The creative chaos of scrappy wonky blocks is enhanced by balancing the wonkiness with beautifully tidy borders. Whether you square up to fit a block size or leave the wonkiness intact with a frame that is then squared up, the end result gives the scrappy wonky creation a setting that lets the wonk shine. The *Place* quilt (page 115) is a perfect example of squaring up and framing in one project.

Squaring Up

Squaring up a block means trimming the last round or layer to fit the trimmed measurements for a block. For these, the size of the block is determined by the size needed for the finished project, and all the wonkiness is in the layers and rounds before the last layer or round. For example, for a 10½″ × 10½″ (25.4 × 25.4cm) Love Shack block (page 45), the final round fits within that 10½″ × 10½″ (25.4 × 25.4cm) square,

ensuring that once the outside ¼″ (6mm) seam allowance is sewn, the final round is still visible. The same applies to blocks like Drunken Pineapple (page 57) and Fly Away Home (page 55). If the trimmed size results in the final rounds or layers being eaten up in the seam allowance, all of your color and wonkiness choices for those last pieces will be erased. For projects like *Night Roost* (page 109), the starting square *and* the final layer are vital to the overall effect of the finished piece, but both could be eaten up in the seam allowance if you don't pay careful attention to their size and width.

Framing Single Blocks

On the other hand, *framing* allows the wonk of a block to be preserved by making the last round or layers a different color than the overall color scheme of the blocks. Often, this color is a background color that connects all the blocks of a project. This choice gives the blocks the look of floating in a frame of the background color while preserving their wonkiness because the

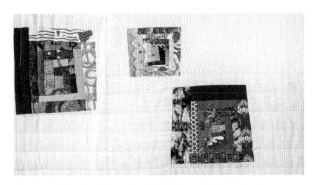

last rounds or layers of the block itself are not squared up—only the framing fabric is. Going back to our example of the *Place* quilt (page 115), some blocks were intentionally made smaller than others and then framed in a creamy off-white fabric that is the unifying background fabric for the quilt. That same quilt includes single- and double-framed blocks where multiple blocks were framed in background fabric, sewn together, and then trimmed to the final larger block size. The smaller blocks float in the light-colored fabric, making their uniqueness stand out and truly shine through.

HOW MUCH BACKGROUND FABRIC IS NEEDED FOR FRAMING?

For a quilt such as *Place* (page 115), where we are framing blocks with a background fabric that is all the same color, we generally buy as much fabric as it would take to cover the entire quilt. Will there be scraps? Yes. But the way the framing is done will result in odd cuts that can be used to frame other blocks. For *Place*, we used about 6 yards (5.5m) of fabric and saved the odd cuts and scraps for other blocks ... and to enhance our scrap collection for future projects!

For our example, we are using the Love Shack (page 45) block, but framing can be used on any block for design purposes, to fit into a larger project, or just because! At the end of the day, framing is a design element and a useful tool. But, sometimes we also do things just for the wonk of it. And that is reason enough.

Follow the steps below for any block. Be sure that the block to be framed is smaller than the trimmed block size for the project so you have room for framing.

1. Choose a background fabric that suits the block and the overall project. For the *Place* quilt, we used a soft white background fabric to allow the blocks to shine.

2. Choose a framing style from the options on these pages and then follow the remaining steps.

Centered-ish

In this example, a Love Shack block is framed on all four sides. This is identical to placing a border around a finished quilt, except that you choose exactly how the block will float within the finished panel. *Figs. A–C*

1. Sew strips of framing fabric to the top. Trim the seam allowance, if needed, and press the seams to one side.

2. Sew strips of framing fabric to one side. Trim the seam allowance, if needed, and press the seams to one side.

3. Continue in this manner until all sides are framed.

4. Square up the block.

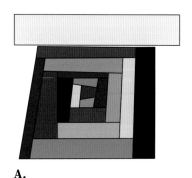

A.

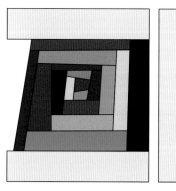

B.

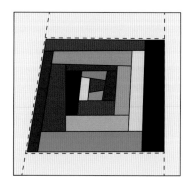

C.

Three-Sided

Next, a Love Shack block is framed on three sides. The edge of the block becomes part of the fourth side. The initial block can sit on any of the four edges, floating within the finished panel. *Figs. D–F*

1. Sew strips of framing fabric to 2 sides. Trim the seam allowance, if needed, and press the seams to one side.

2. Sew strips of framing fabric to the remaining side. Trim the seam allowance, if needed, and press.

3. Square up the block.

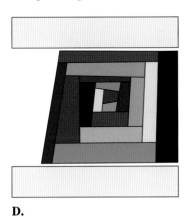

D.

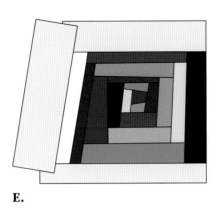

E.

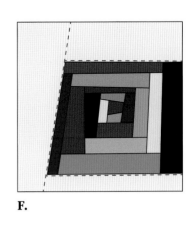

F.

Two-Sided

Here, we have two-sided framing, a Love Shack block framed on two sides. The block sits in the corner (any of the four corners will work). *Figs. G–I*

1. Sew strips of framing fabric to one side. Trim the seam allowance, if needed, and press the seams to one side.

2. Sew strips of framing fabric to the remaining side. Trim the seam allowance, if needed, and press.

3. Square up the block.

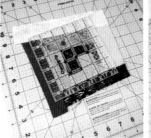

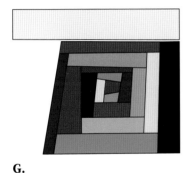

G.

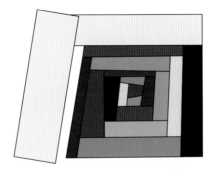

H.

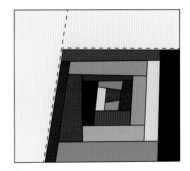

I.

PHOTO OPPORTUNITY

We highly recommend that you use your mobile device or tablet to take note of the layout and measurements needed for your framing pieces and to decide the order of assembly for framing. Here, we took a photo of the position of the Love Shack block under the quilting square and used our mobile device's editing feature to draw in and number the framing pieces. We then took note of the general measurements, using the number of the framing pieces as a reference.

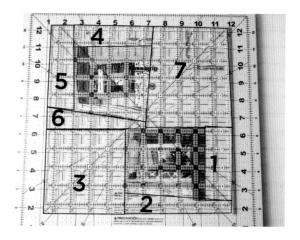

Framing Combo Blocks

At times, some of us become so enamored with the shape of a block that we can't bear the thought of changing it to square it up. When that happens, adding framing around the block allows for that squaring up while leaving the wonkiness undisturbed. In addition, framing provides a resting place for the eye. We make no bones about the fact that we wholly embrace the creative chaos in our creative and personal lives. That said, myriad chaotic colors and shapes in a project can benefit from a less riotous backdrop, providing the eyes a quiet place to rest. Framing provides that respite for the eyes in the same way a mat board allows the details of a photograph to stand out.

Framing can be done on a single block, or two blocks can be framed up into one combo block.

Single block framing – Love Shack block framed in a solid color fabric

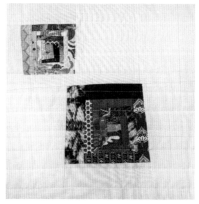

Combo block framing – Being all fancy with two blocks in one frame

A combo block is created when two or more blocks are framed together to make a single, larger block. This is accomplished by creating two blocks that fit inside a larger single block and then filling the empty space with filler fabric or a background fabric. This is an evolved version of framing and adds another element of depth and complexity to the composition of a project.

Two Scrappy Wonky Rose blocks (page 59) are framed with additional wonky green scraps to make one larger combo block.

Three Love Shack (page 45) blocks are framed together to form one larger combo block.

In this example, we use two smaller wonky blocks together to make a larger block. We connect them by using the three-sided method from before (page 33). *Figs. J–M*

1. Make 2 blocks, ensuring that they both fit within the dimensions of the desired trimmed block.

2. Measure the empty space surrounding both blocks, making note of those dimensions and adding ½″ (1.2cm) for seam allowance. Note: We add a little more to ensure that we have some wiggle room for the final trim size.

3. Frame 2 blocks by following the three-sided instructions (page 33).

4. Add a strip to connect the 2 blocks.

5. Use a quilting square to trim to the finished size.

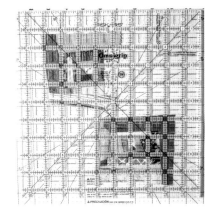

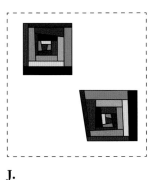

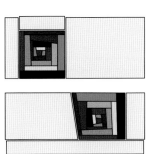

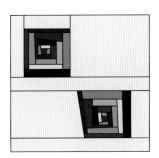

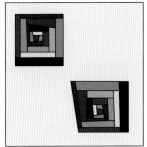

J.   **K.**   **L.**   **M.**

TIME TO GET SCRAPPY!

The blocks in this book are presented first by technique and then by concentration level to give you the best chance for success. If you have not spent enough time sewing to feel confident about jumping right into a Drunken Pineapple block (page 57), create some Good Neighbors (page 40) and All-Seeing Eye (page 43) blocks until you are more comfortable with the scrappy wonkiness. Smaller projects, like pillows, coasters, and placemats, are also great first-time projects to test the wonky waters without a huge commitment of time and concentration. We always like to say, "Give yourself the easy victory to start." Once you are ready to tackle something more involved, start with some strips of fabric and sew them together, then add a different assembly technique to each previous block until you have made all the blocks in this book, and TA-DA you'll have your sampler ... well ... almost. Make your favorites a few more times, and *then* you'll have your sampler.

Here's how we've organized the blocks: We begin with strip piecing and then advance to square stack-and-bridge construction. We then move on to cornered stack-and-bridge construction, which evolves into spirals. The final blocks are stack and slash and Nine-Patch. To further aid your progress, the instructions for each block include an assembled photo as well as a numbered assembly guide to follow until you are ready to freestyle. Working through each of the blocks will develop your piecing skills until even the most complex blocks make sense and can be achieved with minimal wailing and gnashing of teeth. We have broken the list of blocks down and included these headers on the following pages.

That said ... the best advice we can give you is to not try to make a block with a targeted size the first time. Instead, just dive in and start sewing pieces of fabric together.

Strips

These blocks are a great way to dive into the idea of scrappy wonky piecing because all you have to do is sew strips of fabric together in no particular order and not pay attention to width. Use this opportunity to let go of the need to measure every single piece of fabric to within a nanometer of a set pattern.

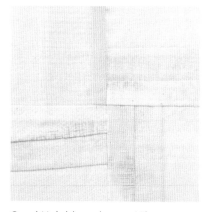

Good Neighbors (page 40)

All-Seeing Eye (page 43)

Square Stack and Bridge

Stack and bridge is a building technique where new pieces of fabric are placed onto the pieces that were just sewn together. For square stack and bridge, the pieces are used to square off the ends of the previously sewn blocks. Place the new piece squarely on the ends of the pieces just sewn together (stack) and ensure that the new piece lays across all the end pieces (bridge).

Love Shack (page 45)

Steppin' Up (page 47)

Down on the Corner (page 49)

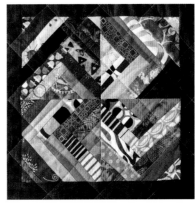

Entwined (page 51)

Cornered Stack and Bridge

These blocks use the stack-and-bridge method for building blocks, but with an added twist. Along with stacking squarely, there's an additional element of stacking a new piece of fabric across a corner created by the previously sewn pieces, creating a squared-off corner. Practice this with Fly Away Home and then move on to Drunken Pineapple.

Fly Away Home (page 55)

Drunken Pineapple (page 57)

Spiral

The creation of the Scrappy Wonky Rose is really more of a guided improv technique where strips of fabric are placed at an angle around a central point and sewn into place. It incorporates elements of stack and bridge and strips, but the new fabric strips are placed at an angle, creating the spiral effect.

Scrappy Wonky Rose (page 59)

Stack and Slash

Stack and slash is a quick method for creating multiple blocks at one time. For our blocks, we place two squares of contrasting colors on top of one another and cut according to the pattern. The pieces are then swapped and sewn together. Two blocks, one set of cuts!

Don Quixote (page 62)

Wonky Nine-Patch (page 64)

Nine-Patch

The description is right there in the name: A Nine-Patch is made up of nine pieces sewn together. Nothing more to it!

Oh, My Stars! (page 66)

FOR THE JOY OF MAKING A THING

There doesn't always have to be a purpose for the thing you are making. Maybe you really love how that block turned out, but it doesn't fit the project you are working on. What if that Scrappy Wonky Rose block you made isn't the size you were aiming for, or you love how it looks without being squared up? No worries! That's the joy of creative chaos. Our walls are covered with one-offs, and even more of them fill boxes in our studio that we take out and display or look at just because. Turn these one-offs into little gems with finished edges of their own or incorporate them into your mending and boro and sashiko projects. What you make can bring you joy without having a specific purpose. Just because.

Good Neighbors

Good fences make good neighbors ... at least that's what they say. This is our take on a rail fence block, and the saying is about fences and neighbors, so that's why we named it that. See, we think we're funny ... so y'all should play along. (*ahem*) Good Neighbors is a compound Four-Patch block made up of smaller component blocks, created with wonky strips of fabric of varying widths and an endless combination of colors.

Below, we present two versions of the Good Neighbors block in a Four-Patch block, with the assembled blocks squared or tipped on a 30°-ish angle.

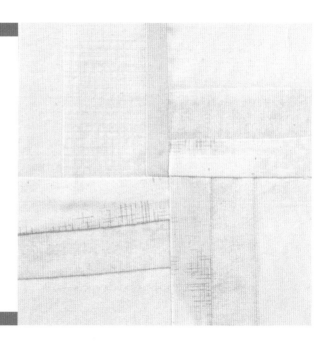

MATERIALS

Various scraps in lengths that diagonally cover your selected block

Square quilting ruler in the sizes of the final trimmed blocks

CUTTING

Various lengths and widths of strips in different colors, patterns, or textures

CONSTRUCTION

All seam allowances are ¼″ (6mm) unless otherwise noted.

Square Good Neighbors

To determine the size of each component block, see Four-Patch Calculations (page 29). Because we are using wonky strips, we make our component blocks about a half inch larger than required and then trim them to the correct size. This ensure that we have enough wiggle room to trim so we don't miss an edge and need to remake a block. This extra ½″ (1.2cm) is completely optional, so it is not included in the instructions.

The Square Good Neighbors block is made up of four component blocks that are each rotated a quarter turn from the previous block and then sewn together. It is shown here as the background for *The Rose Tattoo* (page 127).

For the finished 10″ × 10″ (25.4 × 25.4cm) Square Good Neighbors block for *The Full Monty* quilt (page 112), start by making 4 component blocks that are each 5½″ × 5½″ (14 × 14cm), sew them together, and trim to 10½″ × 10½″ (26.7 × 26.7cm).

Square Good Neighbors Block Construction

1. Place 2 strips with right sides together, sewing down one long side. Strips should be long enough to cover and overlap the edges of the component block template. *Fig. A*

2. Flip open and press the seams to one side.

3. Continue sewing strips until the component block is slightly larger than the size required. *Fig. B*

4. Repeat Steps 1–3 until 4 component blocks have been created.

5. Trim the 4 component blocks with a square template. *Fig. C*

6. Lay the blocks out, turning each one a quarter turn and progressing clockwise. *Fig. D*

7. Sew the top 2 pieces together (right sides facing) along the trimmed edges. Flip open and press the seams to one side. *Fig. E*

8. Sew the bottom 2 pieces together (right sides facing) along the trimmed edges. Flip open and press the seams to one side. *Fig. F*

9. Sew the top and bottom together (right sides facing) along the trimmed edge, being sure to nest the center seams (see Nesting, page 20). Flip open and press the seams to one side, spinning the centers to reduce bulk (see Pressing Matters, page 19). *Fig. G*

10. Trim the edges with a square quilting ruler.

11. Repeat Steps 1–10 for the number of blocks needed for the project.

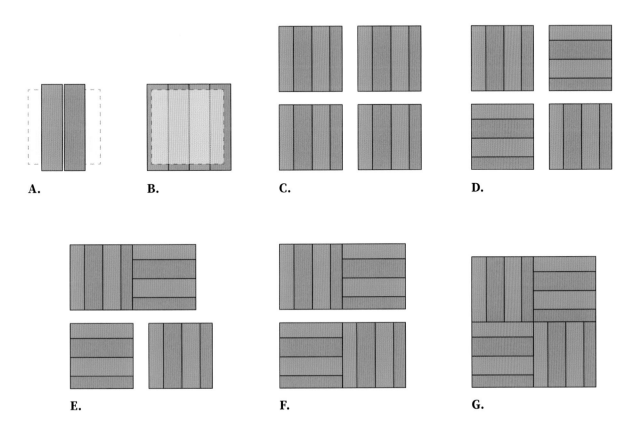

A.   **B.**   **C.**   **D.**

E.   **F.**   **G.**

Wonked Good Neighbors

The Wonked Good Neighbors block, pictured here, is constructed the same as the Square Good Neighbors Block, but with larger component blocks to accommodate the trim size needed to turn the assembled Four-Patch on a 30°-ish angle before trimming the square.

To create a Wonked Good Neighbors block, start with a trimmed Square Good Neighbors block that is 2½″ (6.4cm) larger than the desired size of the trimmed block.

For example, to create a trimmed 10½″ × 10½″ (26.7 × 26.7cm) Wonked Good Neighbors block, first make a trimmed 13″ × 13″ (33 × 33cm) Square Good Neighbors block, turn the 10½″ × 10½″ (26.7 × 26.7cm) square template to about 30°, and trim the excess.

For the finished 10″ (25.4cm) Wonked Good Neighbors Block for The Full Monty quilt

1. Start by making 4 component blocks that are each 7″ × 7″ (17.8 × 17.8cm), as shown in the Square Good Neighbors Block instructions (page 41). *Fig. H*

2. Sew the 4 component blocks together to make a 13½″ × 13½″ (34.3 × 34.3cm) Square Good Neighbors block. *Fig. I*

3. Place the 10½″ × 10½″ (26.7 × 26.7cm) square quilting ruler on the assembled block and turn it about 30°. *Fig. J*

4. Trim to 10½″ × 10½″ (26.7 × 26.7cm). *Fig. K*

Repeat Steps 1–4 for the number of blocks needed for the project.

TIP • Keep going!

For larger projects, rather than making each Good Neighbors block one at a time, we like to prepare a pile of strips to make a stack of component blocks (as many as we need for the project). Then, we trim them all and, finally, sew them all together into finished blocks. This saves time because we don't lose focus by continually jumping back and forth between different tasks.

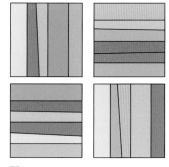

H.

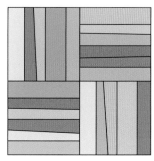

I.

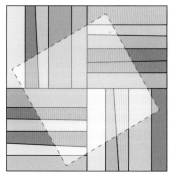

J.

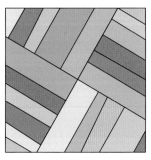

K.

All-Seeing Eye

Fall deep into the mesmeric depths of the all-seeing eye! We fell in love with this style of block while teaching our quilt-as-you-go classes, so it was a must to bring along in scrappy wonky style. Try pop-of-color centers to ground your creations and don't shy away from monochromatic and gradient color schemes.

The All-Seeing Eye block is a four-square block made up of strips of fabric of varying widths. Strips are arranged on a diagonal square and then attached to make the final trimmed block. For a 10½″ × 10½ (26.7 × 26.7cm) trimmed block, you will need 4 blocks that are each 5½″ × 5½″ (14 × 14 cm).

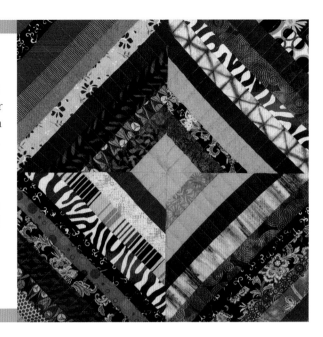

MATERIALS

Various scraps in lengths that diagonally cover your selected block

Template slightly larger than needed for your component block (for example, 6″ × 6″ template is required for a 5½″ × 5½″ [14 × 14 cm] finished block)

Square quilting ruler in the sizes of the final trimmed blocks (for example, 5½″ × 5½″ [14 × 14cm], 10½″ × 10½″ [26.7 × 26.7cm])

CUTTING

Various lengths and widths of strips in different colors, patterns, or textures

CONSTRUCTION

All seam allowances are ¼″ (6mm) unless otherwise noted.

1. Arrange strips on the template so they fit diagonally (point to point). Stack strips in the order you want to sew them. Make sure to allow for enough seam allowance and overhang.

2. Set aside and repeat 3 times for a total of 4 blocks.

Initial layout for the All-Seeing Eye

TIP • Aim Big

Like in the Good Neighbors block, to create a final 10½″ × 10½″ (26.7 × 26.7cm) trimmed block, we use a 6″ × 6″ (15.2 × 15.2cm) square ruler for laying out the strips on each component block and initial trimming. This gives us enough room to trim the final composite block without accidentally coming up with a short side. Make a template the size of your component blocks to ensure that you don't make blocks that are too small to complete your larger block.

ANOTHER TIP • Color

Assemble strips so a pop of color appears in the center of the finished eye.

3. Place 2 strips with right sides together, with the longer one centered on the shorter one. *Fig. A*

4. Sew to attach.

5. Flip open and press the seam to one side. *Fig. B*

6. Continue in the same manner until the block is assembled. Stop every so often to use your square template to check that the block is becoming the correct size. You may need to add or remove strips.

7. Square up your block with a square quilting ruler. *Fig. C*

8. Repeat for the remaining 3 blocks.

9. Lay out the 4 blocks so they create the "eye." *Fig. D*

10. Place the top 2 blocks together, right sides facing, and sew the seam. *Fig. E*

11. Flip over and press the seam to one side.

12. Place the bottom 2 blocks together, right sides facing, and sew the seam. *Fig. F*

13. Flip over and press the seam to one side.

14. Place the top and bottom pieces together, right sides facing, and sew the seam. *Fig. G*

15. Turn and press the seams one more time.

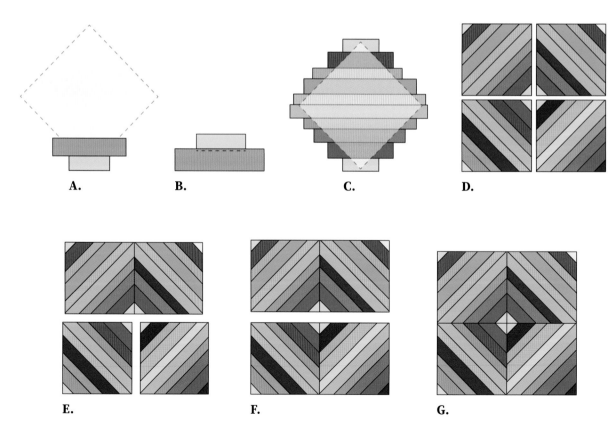

A.   B.   C.   D.

E.   F.   G.

Love Shack

We fondly remember nights in the clubs dancing with wild abandon to that song and stopping to scream *tiiiiiin roof, rusted!* at the top of our lungs. We're not really log-cabin-in-the-woods kind of folx (how far away is the nearest downtown shopping core?), so a more urban version of the classic in our scrappy wonky style is our new groove.

Love Shack blocks are created by using the stack-and-bridge method of construction (page 37). Each block is built in a spiral pattern from the center out, one side at a time, making it ultimately customizable for shape and size. The possibilities for color combos and wonk are nearly endless. Go with a predetermined color palette or let the scraps fall where they may. Build layers toward a predetermined size or let the wonk lead where it will. This block is forgiving and empowering at the same time.

We highly recommend making the first few Love Shack blocks without paying attention to the finished size. Let them develop organically and see what happens. Our first few blocks *ever* are in the *Place* quilt (page 115). We framed them (see Framing, page 31) and combined them into combo blocks (page 34) to preserve their natural wonky beauty.

MATERIALS

Generous supply of scrap fabric

Square quilting ruler for checking size and squaring up

CUTTING

Various lengths and widths of strips in different colors, patterns, or textures

CONSTRUCTION

All seam allowances are ¼˝ (6mm) unless otherwise noted.

1. Working from the center out, place the first 2 square-ish blocks (Piece 1 and Piece 2) together by lining up 1 side on each block. Don't worry if they don't line up perfectly or aren't exactly the same size. Go with the wonk! Note: The size of these 2 blocks is up to you. We recommend starting with square-ish shapes that are about ¾˝ to 1˝ (1.9 to 2.5cm) across … or so. Don't overthink it. The larger the initial blocks are, the larger your final block will most likely end up.

2. With right sides facing, sew Piece 1 and Piece 2 together. Trim off any excess fabric from the seam allowance and top and bottom edges, if needed. Press the seams to the outside of the block. *Fig. A*

3. Now, lay a longer strip across the top of Piece 1 and Piece 2 so it bridges both pieces. Trim your strip to rough length. This is Piece 3.

4. As in Step 2, sew Piece 3 to Piece 1/2 trim the seam allowance, and press toward what will be the outside edge. *Fig. B*

5. Continue working in a spiral, either to the right or the left, to add Piece 4 to the side of the previously sewn piece, as shown. Make sure that the piece is long enough to bridge the ends of 2 of the previously sewn pieces. Sew, trim, and press. *Fig. C*

6. Continuing to work in the same spiral direction, add Piece 5 to the previously sewn piece. Note: You are now bridging the ends of 3 pieces rather than 2 as in the previous steps. From this point on, *you will always be bridging across the ends of three pieces.* This is how you will keep track of where you are in your spiral. If you see 3 ends to bridge, you are on the right track. Only see 2 ends to bridge? You've started working in reverse. If you are doing this type of stacked spiral construction for the first time, check twice before you sew. *Fig. D*

7. Keep working in a spiral, bridging the next piece onto the previously sewn piece and other 2 open sides. Remember: You are looking for 3 ends to bridge. Keep working outward until your block is large enough for your purposes. *Figs. E–G*

TIP • Wonk It Up!

As you test the layout of each piece being added to the block, check how your "wonk" is going. You can adjust the amount of wonk by changing the angle of each piece as you sew it on (see Wonk It Up, page 28).

8. Now that you have all your pieces attached and your Love Shack block is complete, clean up the edges with a ruler and a rotary cutter. If you need squared blocks and do not want to use framing, trim your edges square with a square quilting ruler. *Fig. H*

If you are using the smaller blocks framed or in a combo block, trim the edges straight, but leave the angles as wonky as you like. *Fig. I*

9. Repeat Steps 1–8 to create as many blocks as needed for the size of your project.

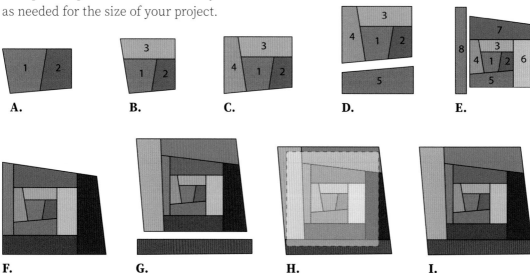

A.   **B.**   **C.**   **D.**   **E.**

F.   **G.**   **H.**   **I.**

Steppin' Up

The first image that popped into our geeky brains when we looked at our first finished Steppin' Up block? Step pyramids! Thus, Steppin' Up was born. Like Love Shack and Drunken Pineapple, this block is screaming for color palette play. Steppin' Up blocks are a natural progression of the Love Shack block and are created using the same stack-and-bridge method of construction. The block is worked from the center out, beginning with a square-ish block, and strips are added—two sides at a time—on opposite sides of the starting block, bridging the previously sewn pieces.

MATERIALS

Generous pile of scraps

Square quilting ruler for checking size and squaring up

CUTTING

Various lengths and widths of strips in different colors, patterns, or textures

CONSTRUCTION

All seam allowances are ¼″ (6mm) unless otherwise noted.

The construction of Steppin' Up blocks is as follows: Pieces 2 and 3 are attached to the left and right sides of Piece 1, each seam is pressed, and any excess at the seam is trimmed. Next, Pieces 4 and 5 are placed on the top and bottom of the previous blocks, again so each bridges the span of the previously sewn pieces. This can be straight across or as wonky as you like.

1. Working from the center out and starting with 1 center, square-ish block (Piece 1), place strips (Piece 2 and Piece 3) along opposite sides of Piece 1. *Fig. A* Note: The size of the center block is up to you. We recommend starting with square-ish shapes that are about ¾″ to 1″ (1.9 to 2.5cm) across ... or so. Don't overthink it. The larger these initial blocks are, the larger your final block will most likely end up.

2. With right sides facing, sew Piece 2 and Piece 3 to the opposite sides of Piece 1. Trim any excess fabric from the seam allowance, as needed. Press the seams toward the outside. *Fig. B*

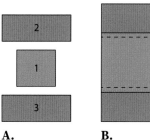

A.   **B.**

3. Now, lay two longer strips (Piece 4 and Piece 5) along the opposite remaining 2 sides of Piece 1, ensuring that they bridge the full length of Piece ½/₃. *Fig. C*

4. With right sides facing, sew Piece 4 and Piece 5 into place. Trim any excess fabric from the seam allowance and press the seam outward. *Fig. D*

5. Continue to work in the same manner, adding 2 strips to the opposite sides, bridging the ends of previously sewn strips. As always, adjust the wonk as needed to suit your personal taste. Keep working outward until your block is large enough for the project ... or until it makes you happy. You can always frame it or make a combo block with it later. *Fig. E*

6. Once you have all your pieces attached and your Steppin' Up block is complete, clean up the edges with a ruler and a rotary cutter.

If you need squared blocks and do not want to use framing, trim your edges square with a square quilting ruler. If you are using the smaller blocks framed or as part of a combo block, trim the edges straight, but leave the angles as wonky as you like.

Repeat Steps 1–6 to create as many blocks as needed for the project.

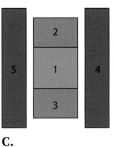

C.

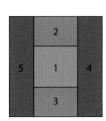

D.

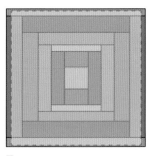

E.

Down on the Corner

Think of a Love Shack block built diagonally outward from one corner. Can you tell yet that music plays a huge part in our lives? Use these in a squared layout like we do in *The Full Monty* quilt (page 112), but look for these to pop up in an on-point layout in *Feywild* (page 136). Down on the Corner blocks are created by using the stack-and-bridge method of construction. For this block, start with a square and add strips to the left and top sides only, bridging the previously sewn pieces. Continue in this manner until the block is the size required for your needs.

MATERIALS

Generous pile of scraps

Square quilting ruler for checking size and squaring up

CUTTING

Various lengths and widths of strips in different colors, patterns, or textures

CONSTRUCTION

All seam allowances are ¼″ (6mm) unless otherwise noted.

The construction of Down on the Corner blocks is as follows: Piece 2 is attached to the top side of Piece 1; each seam is pressed, and any excess at the seam is trimmed. Next, Piece 3 is placed along the left side, bridging the previous pieces (see Terminology, page 25). Each strip can be straight across or as wonky as you like (see Wonk It Up!, page 28).

1. Begin with 1 center, square-ish starting block (Piece 1); lay a strip (Piece 2) along the top of the block and trim it slightly longer than the side of Piece 1. *Fig. A*

NOTE • Starting Block

The size of the starting block is important only in that it should be large enough so it isn't completely eaten up in the seam allowance when you're sewing blocks together or adding sashing. We recommend starting blocks that are at least 1½″ × 1½″ (3.8 × 3.8cm) ... or so. Don't overthink it. Play with the starting block size to see what you prefer.

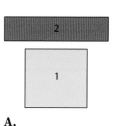

A.

2. With right sides facing, sew Piece 2 in place, trim any excess fabric from the seam allowance, and press the seams outward. *Fig. B*

3. Next, lay a strip (Piece 3) along one side of the existing sewn block and trim it slightly longer than the side of Piece 1/2. *Fig. C*

4. With right sides facing, sew Piece 3 to the side of the existing block, bridging both edges. Trim off any excess fabric from the seam allowance, as needed. Press the seams toward the outside.

5. Continue to work in the same pattern, with 1 strip to the top side bridging previous rows and then another on the left side, adjusting the wonk as needed and trimming excess before pressing the seams to the outside. Keep working outward until your block is the size needed for the project. *Fig. D*

6. Once you have all your pieces attached and your Down on the Corner block is complete, square the block by using a square ruler and rotary cutter. *Fig. E*

Repeat Steps 1–6 to create as many blocks as needed for the size of your quilt.

NOTE • Wonk It Up!
Down on the Corner is a great candidate for leaving the edges wonky and using framing. Mix and match squared and framed blocks for added visual effect.

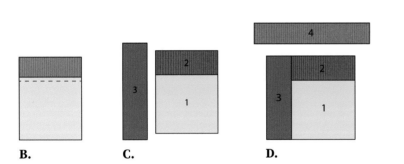

B.   C.   D.

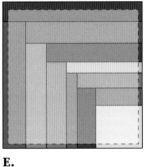

E.

Entwined

If you rotate the construction for Down on the Corner so the starting point is the center of the block, the result is a block that can be contained in a set square, combined in a Four-Patch, or turned into a panel of any length or width. Check out the single block and Four-Patch versions in *The Full Monty* quilt (page 112) and the longer panels in the *Upson Downs* throw (page 121) and the *Totes Cute Tote* (page 100).

Entwined is similar to Down on the Corner in that it begins with a square and adds strips to the sides only, bridging the previously sewn pieces until the block is the desired length. For Entwined blocks, the starting square is cut in half diagonally and placed at the bottom center of the block being made. For Entwined panels, such as the *Totes Cute Tote* and the *Upson Downs* throw, a full starting square is used, and the strips are placed by working outward in both directions, using the starting square as a feature point.

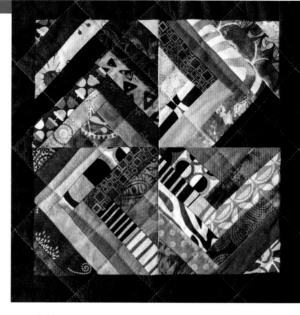

TIP • Compound Blocks

Entwined blocks make FAB compound blocks! Try making smaller blocks to assemble into larger blocks—for example, 4 blocks that are each 5½″ × 5½″ (14 × 14cm) sewn together make up the 10½″ × 10½″ (26.7 × 26.7cm) block used in *The Full Monty* quilt (page 112).

Four smaller blocks making a compound block

MATERIALS

Generous pile of scrap fabric

Quilting ruler for checking size and squaring up

Starting Square: We use a starting square for each block or panel that is the finished width of the final block or panel, divided by 2. For example, for a 6½″-wide (16.5cm) block or panel that would be finished at 6″ (15.2cm), we would use a 3″ × 3″ (7.6 × 7.6cm) starting square. For a 4½″-wide (11.4cm) block or panel that would be finished at 4″ (10cm), we would use a 2″ × 2' (5 × 5cm) starting square. You are, of course, free to use larger or smaller starting blocks, depending on the look you prefer, and, of course, all measurements are ish.

CUTTING

Various scraps in your favorite colors/patterns

For the length of the strips, take the trimmed width of the block and add 1″ (2.5cm). For example, for a 5½″-wide (14cm) block, we would use 6½″ (16.5cm) strips. The same applies to making the braids panels, like those used in the *Upson Downs* throw (page 121) and the *Totes Adorbs Tote* (page 100).

The width of the strips can vary; we use strips that are 1″–2½″ (2.5–6.4cm) wide. For shorter blocks, we can get away with using random widths, but be warned … once you start making wider strips, you need to remember that the two sides must balance, or your braid panel will be heavily skewed to one side or the other and won't square up properly.

CONSTRUCTION

All seam allowances are ¼″ (6mm) unless otherwise noted.

Blocks

1. Cut the starting square in half diagonally to create a half-square triangle (Piece 1). Turned on point, this triangle will be the center of the block. *Fig. A*

2. Next, place a strip (Piece 2) along one side of the triangle. This strip will be trimmed, so a little overhang is okay. *Fig. B*

3. With right sides facing, sew Piece 2 into place, trim any uneven edges from the seam allowance, and press the seam outward. *Fig. C*

4. Next, place a new strip (Piece 3) along the opposite side, being sure to bridge (see Terminology, page 25) the triangle and the end of the strip just sewn. *Fig. D*

5. Sew, trim, and press as before.

6. Continue sewing strips in this manner, alternating sides until the desired length is reached. *Fig. E*

7. Clean up the edges of the block by using a ruler or quilting template. *Fig. F*

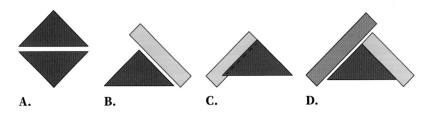

A.   B.   C.   D.

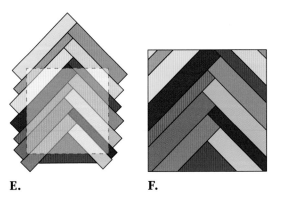

E.   F.

Panels

Generally, the construction of Entwined panels, like those used in the *Totes Cute Tote* and the *Upson Downs* throw, is the same as for the blocks. The notable exception is that the starting square is not cut in half but, rather, remains a square. After that, strips are sewn in the same manner as blocks until one side of the desired panel length is reached. The panel is turned and strips are sewn again starting on the opposite side of the initial square.

Panels Used in *Upson Downs* Throw

Be careful how wonky your cuts are, especially in long panels, such as in the *Upson Downs* throw. The key to making the longer panels work is that they remain fairly straight, with the center points of the braids aligned as closely as possible to a center line. Will they wander off to the side? Probably. Again, that's the charm of scrappy wonky! That said, don't sweat it too much. Check the center alignment with a quilting ruler, yardstick, or T-square for the longer sections and realign as needed. If your braid panel starts to skew to one side or the other, use a thinner strip on the side it is skewing toward and a thicker strip on the side you want it to correct to. Remeasure for a couple of layers until you are back on course.

A final point to be mindful of with these longer panels is the angles. Although you don't have to fret too awfully about creating precise 45° angles, it's a good idea to visually check for the right angles as you go. If it looks like the angles are starting to spread or crunch up too much, adjust a little at a time until you are back to right-ish angles. Remember, this isn't about precision cutting ... let it happen and adjust as needed (if needed), and everything will work out beautifully.

A construction note for making panels that have a center starting block is to balance both sides of the panel so the strips overlap alternatively rather than from one direction of the panel overlapping the other.

1. Cut the center square and turn it on point. *Fig. A*

2. Add strips on opposite sides of 1 of the points, just as you would for an Entwined block. *Fig. B*

3. Now, add strips on 2 sides of the opposite point. These new strips should overlap the first 2 strips. *Fig. C*

4. Repeat Steps 2–3, alternating sides until both directions of the panel have several layers of strips. *Fig. D*

5. Continue to add strips to 1 end of the panel until the desired length is achieved. *Fig. E*

6. Add strips to the opposite end of the panel until the desired length is achieved. *Fig. F*

7. Use a straight edge to trim the edges of the panel to the width in the project instructions. *Fig. G*

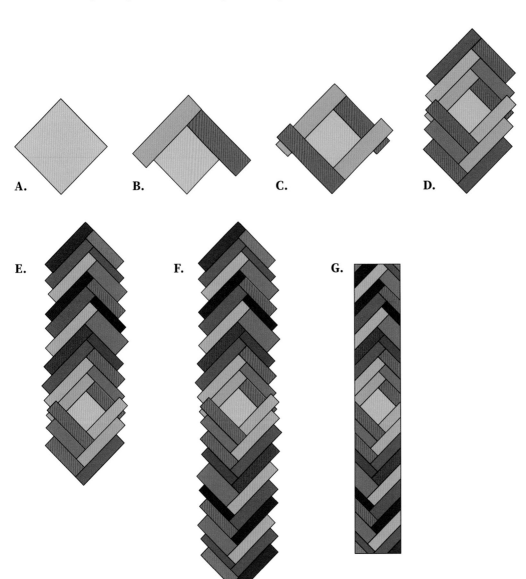

A.   B.   C.   D.

E.   F.   G.

Fly Away Home

What do you get when Down on the Corner meets a Drunken Pineapple? To us, this evokes birds taking wing on a catty-corner flight path. Fly Away Home caps the corners of a Down on the Corner block and is prime practice material for a Drunken Pineapple. The imagery of birds flying in formation was our inspiration for the *Night Roost* wall hanging (page 109). These blocks also provide directional movement toward the four corners of *The Full Monty* quilt (page 112).

Close up of the "Birds" in *Night Roost*

MATERIALS

Random scraps for the blocks

Single color or pattern of fabric for the "birds"

Square quilting ruler for checking size and squaring up

CUTTING

A starting square-ish shape approximately 1½"–1¾"-ish (3.8–4.4cm), depending on the size of the finished block

Various lengths and widths of strips in different colors, patterns, or textures

CONSTRUCTION

All seam allowances are ¼" (6mm) unless otherwise noted.

1. Begin with 1 starter square-ish (Piece 1); lay a longer strip (Piece 2) across 1 side of the block and trim to a length slightly longer than the side of Piece 1. *Fig. A*

> **NOTE • Starting Block**
> The size of the starting block is important only in that it should be large enough so it isn't completely eaten up in the seam allowance when sewing blocks together or adding sashing. We recommend starting blocks that are at least 1½" × 1½" (3.8 × 3.8cm) square … or so. Don't overthink it. Play with the starting block size to see what you prefer.

2. With right sides facing, sew Piece 2 in place, trim any excess fabric from the seam allowance, and press the seams outward. *Fig. B*

A.   **B.**

3. Next, lay a strip (Piece 3) across the top of the existing sewn block and trim to a length slightly longer than the top side of Piece 1/2. This is Piece 3.

4. With right sides facing, sew Piece 3 to the top of the existing block, bridging both edges. Trim off any excess fabric from the seam allowance as needed. Press the seams toward the outside. *Fig. C*

5. To ensure that the tip of the starting square is not covered up by the next piece, trim the corner created by the 2 strips to about ¼" (6mm) from the tip. Adjust the wonk as you like by adding a slight tilt to one side or the other of this trim cut. *Fig. D*

6. Lay a "bird strip" (Piece 4) across the just-trimmed corner edge.

7. With right sides facing, sew the "bird strip" in place.

8. Press the seam to one side and trim any excess; use the corner of a square quilting template to create a clean point. Remember, you will be removing ¼" (6mm) from the width of the strips/point with the next set of strips, so trim judiciously.

9. Continue to work in the same pattern, adding 1 strip on the side and top, bridging previous rows, and then adding another to the corner. Adjust the wonk as needed and trim any excess before pressing the seams to the outside. Keep working outward until your block is the desired size. *Fig. E*

> **NOTE • The Size of the Bird**
> The width of the bird strip and the side strips work together to determine how large the bird will be and how wide the strips will be after this trim. We use bird strips that are about 1½"–1¾" (3.8–4.4cm) wide and bird strips that are about 1¾"–2" (4.4–5cm) wide. Again, these are ish measurements, and we have used narrower and wider strips for each, depending on the size of the blocks and the effect of the birds.

10. Once it is large enough, your Fly Away Home block is complete. Clean up the edges with a ruler or square quilting template and rotary cutter. *Fig. F*

11. Repeat Steps 1–10 to create as many blocks as needed for the size of your quilt.

C.

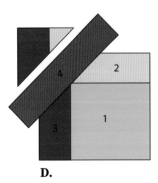

D.

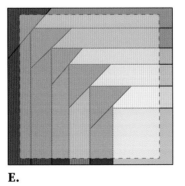

E.

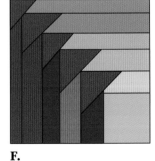

F.

Drunken Pineapple

A favorite summer party treat of ours used to be pineapple chunks soaked for a night (or two) in a lovely rum. Those days are a little past us, but that warm, slightly off-kilter feeling is perfectly captured in the layers of a scrappy wonky pineapple block. This is a stunning block created using a random jumble of colors, or you can play with contrasting lights and darks to give this block a hypnotic vibe. Again, back to that rummy pineapple.

Drunken Pineapple is created by using cornered stack-and-bridge (page 37) construction built from the center out, four sides at a time. The method we use for this block consists of a starting square with half-square triangles attached to all four sides. This is done twice. Then, we continue adding layers with fabric strips, working square across four sides and then turning the block 45° to add strips, capping the points.

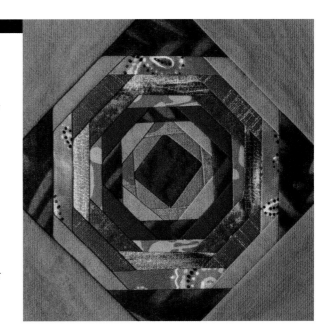

MATERIALS

Plenty of scraps for the blocks, more than you think ...

Square quilting ruler for checking size and squaring up

CUTTING

Cut 1 square-ish shape about ¾″–1¾″-ish (1.9–4.4cm-ish), depending on the size of the finished block you are constructing

Various lengths and widths of strips in different colors, patterns, or textures

CONSTRUCTION

All seam allowances are ¼″ (6mm) unless otherwise noted.

> **NOTE • Square-ish**
> We generally wait until the last round to square up blocks, but if the wonk is wonking a bit too much, we square up (ish) as we go along.

1. Cut 1 center square.

2. Using the center square as a guide, cut 2 slightly larger squares. *Fig. A*

3. Cut the 2 larger squares in half diagonally, creating 4 half square triangles. *Fig. B*

A.

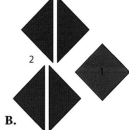

B.

4. Sew the 4 resulting half squares to the flat sides of the center square. *Fig. C*

5. Press the seams to the outside.

6. Lay the new square on 2 more pieces of fabric and cut 2 squares slightly larger than the new square. *Fig. D*

7. Cut the 2 larger squares in half diagonally, creating 4 half squares again. *Fig. E*

8. Sew the 4 resulting half squares to the existing new block along the square sides. The half squares should just touch the tips of the center square. *Fig. F*

9. Press the seams to the outside.

10. Now, sew strips across the 4 points of the square just made. These strips should cover the points of the previous layer. *Fig. G*

11. Continue in this manner, adding strips that cap the ends of the previous layers, until the block is a round or two short of the desired trimmed size. *Fig. H*

12. Use your square ruler to gauge when you are within a round or two of the desired trimmed size. *Fig. I*

> **TIP • Width**
> Use wide enough strips at this point to make sure that the trimmed size fits within the edges of the square ruler and that the block ends with the colors you want and with enough room left for a ¼″ (6mm) seam allowance.

13. Square up the edges of the block with a square ruler. *Fig. J*

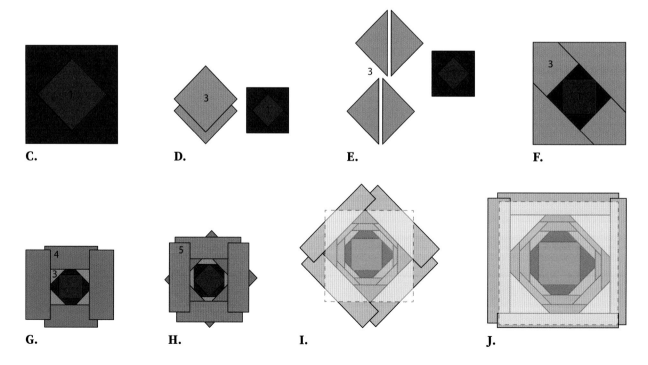

C.   D.   E.   F.

G.   H.   I.   J.

Scrappy Wonky Rose

Not gonna lie—just like the Slinky, Velcro, and X-rays, the Scrappy Wonky Rose block was an accidental discovery. One day, Shannon was playing with a Drunken Pineapple (the block, not the boozy bromeliad), and her wonk went a little too far—as tends to happen with or without the addition of rum. We both agreed that the resulting helical shape looked more like a deconstructed rose than a pineapple. Her observation, hastily thumb-typed into her Notes app one night before bed, became an obsessive session of experimentations with shapes and forms. Thus, the Scrappy Wonky Rose was born.

The creation of the Scrappy Wonky Rose is a guided improv technique where strips of fabric are placed at an angle around a central point and sewn into place. It incorporates elements of stack and bridge and strips, but here, the new fabric strips are placed at an angle, creating a spiral construction.

MATERIALS

Various scraps in shades of your choice. We use yellow for the center block, then reds/oranges for the petals and greens and browns for the leaves. Perhaps a yellow or a blue rose is more to your liking?

Quilting square or template for squaring up

CUTTING

3–4 small pieces of similarly colored fabric (such as yellow), cut into small square-ish shapes for the center block

Lots of random scraps in varying widths and lengths in the colors you want for your roses and greenery

CONSTRUCTION

All seam allowances are ¼″ (6mm) unless otherwise noted.

Notes about the angles: The shallower the angle of the new pieces, the more gradual and smooth the overall spiral will be. We prefer this for the main body of the rose. Deeper angles create a chunky spiral; we prefer this for the greens surrounding the rose. But, in fact, a mix of the two makes a much more natural-looking rose block.

1. Working with yellows, sew 3–4 small pieces of fabric together into a square(ish) shape. The size of these pieces is up to you, but the larger the center is, the larger the flower will most likely be. *Figs. A-B*

2. Once assembled, cut your center into a 5-sided shape. Don't worry about the actual dimensions of each side—just make it 5-sided. *Fig. C*

3. Pick one of the flat 5 sides of the center and sew on 1 piece of "rose" fabric. Trim any excess fabric and press the seam to the outside of the rose.

4. Moving to the next flat side, sew 1 piece of rose fabric, making sure to overlap the new piece with the piece just sewn as well as the flat side, trim, and press the seam to the outside. Continue to sew pieces of the rose until all 5 flat sides have 1 piece. We are not spiraling yet! The width of each rose piece can (and should) vary. That's what will give each rose its own style. *Figs. D-E*

5. Still not spiraling, sew 5 rose pieces along the flat sides of the previous rose layer, being sure to overlap each new piece with the previously sewn pieces. *Figs. F-G*

6. Now, we spiral! Working in one direction, either clockwise or counterclockwise, place a strip of rose fabric on top of the last piece sewn from the previous round. Remember to keep a shallow-ish angle. Play with the placement of the petal piece until you are happy. *Fig. H*

7. Sew into place, trim, and press the seam to the outside of the rose.

8. Choose another piece of rose fabric different in shade, tone, or pattern from the first spiral piece and place it similarly across the first spiral piece as well as the previous round of rose piece.

NOTE • Keep Going!
It usually takes a couple of spiral rounds for the rose shape to start to emerge. This is a trust-the-process technique, so keep going. It is also a very forgiving technique. If the rose isn't shaping up exactly as you wanted, adjust the shape with the next piece or round.

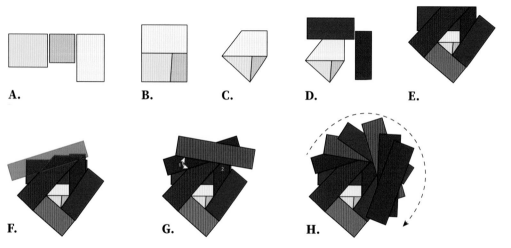

A. **B.** **C.** **D.** **E.**

F. **G.** **H.**

9. Continue with spiral rounds until you are happy with the shape of the rose. Check the size of your rose with a square template occasionally to ensure that there is enough room for greenery.

10. Continue with spiral rounds, using greens and brownish tones. We used wider strips placed on a deeper angle for the greens, giving it a chunkier, leaflike appearance. The amount of green in your block is entirely up to your tastes and will likely change with each Scrappy Wonky Rose block you create. *Fig. I*

11. For square blocks, use a square quilting template to check that your rose is large enough to fill the entire block, and then square up. *Figs. J-K*

For larger roses, like the one we create for the *Pillow Talk* pillow (page 96), the green pieces can become very long. To keep them from going completely off course, we suggest that you lay them out where you want them to be and then pin them in place before sewing. We love the wonky, but too much wonky can make your rose buckle up and warp. One alternative for the green pieces for larger roses is to sew together previously trimmed green pieces in wider strips and chunks.

I.

J.

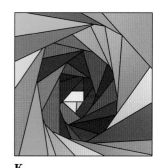

K.

JUST KEEP STITCHING!

Some of these blocks really don't look like much for the first couple of rounds or layers. Especially when you are making them for the first time, this vagueness can be a little alarming. The more rounds and layers you add, the more the final piece will take shape, and you will discover the beautiful chaos of the overall design. *Stitch on!*

Don Quixote

Cervantes gave us the ultimate windmill assailant, and now we present the block that bears the name of that dauntless ingenious gentleman. Fittingly, this block uses a stack, slash, and swap construction method that is quick and to the point and will leave you feeling far more jubilant than our frenzied friend of Rocinante.

The experienced quilter who is used to the exacting measurements of traditional piecing and the rigorous following of templates will find this block to be the perfect place to start their Scrappy Wonky journey. Some traditional measuring and piecing techniques are employed, but we are still dipping our toes into the pool of scrappy wonky "ish measurements" and wonky cutting.

On the other hand, someone who has never sewn one quilt block in their life will find that this is a safe place to start on the scrappy wonky quilt path. There is *some* measuring, but even that can be a bit "ish" because everything will come out fine once the block is squared up.

That said, someone who already enjoys the freedom and creative chaos that come with making scrappy wonky blocks will see that this block requires little thinking and provides immediate results and control of the amount of variation. You could easily prepare an entire quilt's worth of blocks in a day-ish and finish the top in a few days-ish.

Whatever your experience level, take a deep breath and dive in!

MATERIALS

2 colors/patterns cotton fabric for starter blocks

Square quilting ruler for squaring up

CUTTING

2 squares main color

2 squares contrasting color

CONSTRUCTION

All seam allowances are ¼″ (6mm) unless otherwise noted.

Don Quixote is a four-patch compound block made from four wonky-cut component blocks. In addition, we use the stack, slash, and swap technique to make those component blocks. To ensure that everything comes out nice and tidy in the end, we start with a couple of quick calculations.

First, use the Four-Patch Calculations (page 29). Divide the total width of the finished block by the number of component blocks that will make it up and then add ½″ (1.2cm) seam allowance to each of those blocks.

For a 10″ × 10″ (25.4 × 25.4cm) finished block, we need 4 square component blocks that are each 5½″ × 5½″ (14 × 14cm).

Each of those component blocks have 1 cut in them, meaning that they are made up of 2 pieces. Using that same rule, we need to add ¼″ (6mm) for the cut edges, so we add an additional ½″ (1.2cm) to that starter block. Our starter blocks are 6″ × 6″ (15.2 × 15.2cm) square. Now … that seam allowance is going to eat up a little bit of real estate and can cause the component blocks to come out a bit smaller than we need. For that reason, we add another ½″ (1.2cm) of wiggle room to our seam allowances and use 6½″ × 6½″ (16.5 × 16.5cm) starter blocks for our compound blocks to create a finished 10″ × 10″ (25.4 × 25.4cm) Don Quixote block.

10″ × 10″ (25.4 × 25.4cm) Block Construction Example

1. Cut 4 starter blocks, each 6½″ × 6½″ (16.5 × 16.5cm), 2 in the main color and 2 in the contrasting color. *Fig. A*

2. Stack the starter blocks, alternating main color (MC) and contrasting color (CC). *Fig. B*

3. Make 1 shallow diagonal cut. *Fig. C*

4. Lay out the cut blocks in a square formation. *Fig. D*

5. Swap half of the MC pieces with CC pieces, creating the windmill shape. *Fig. E*

6. With right sides facing, sew the diagonal seam on each block. *Fig. F*

7. Sew the sets together, being sure to align the 4 component blocks by the center of the larger block. *Fig. G*

8. Square up to 10½″ × 10½″ (26.7 × 26.7cm). *Fig. H*

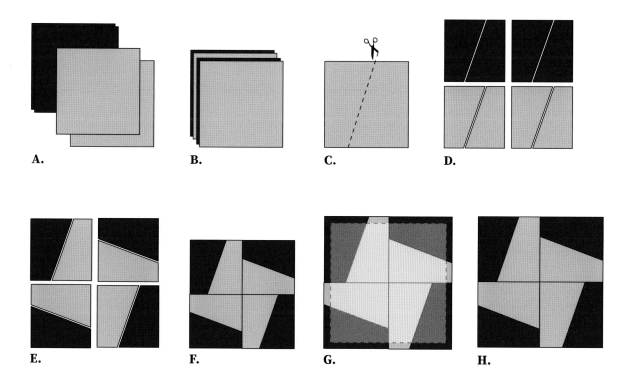

A.   B.   C.   D.

E.   F.   G.   H.

Wonky Nine-Patch

Traditional Nine-Patch blocks are full of exacting measurements and precision sewing, but not so with our wonky version of the nine-pieced wonder. Follow the guide for the starting blocks and then, using the stack, slash, and swap method of construction, quickly create two contrasting blocks. The easily customizable sizing of this block makes it the most versatile of the Nine-Patches.

The joy of making scrappy Wonky Nine-Patch blocks using this stacking method and wonky cuts is that they can be made in any finished size. This flexibility negates the issue of making finished blocks that are only divisible by 3. *Woohoo!* All that's needed is to follow the process we outline in Four-Patch and Nine-Patch Blocks (page 28) to determine the size of the starting block based on how large the finished block is to be.

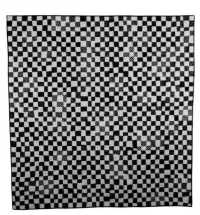

What She Found (page 124) is where you will see just how impactful these nine little patches can be en masse.

Custom sizes that are not divisible by 3 are easy to make with the Wonky Nine-Patch. This is the 5˝ X 5˝ (12.7 × 12.7cm) finished block from the *What She Found* quilt.

How about a Wonky Nine-Patch as a Four-Patch? Here you go! This is the 10˝ × 10˝ (25.4 × 25.4cm) finished block in *The Full Monty* quilt (page 112), created by making 4 Wonky Nine-Patch blocks that are each 5½˝ × 5½˝ (14 × 14cm) and assembling them into a Four-Patch block that is 10½˝ × 10½˝ (26.7 × 26.7cm).

MATERIALS

2 pieces of contrasting fabric

Square quilting ruler for checking size and squaring up

CUTTING

1 starting square

CONSTRUCTION

All seam allowances are ¼″ (6mm) unless otherwise noted.

1. Decide on the finished size of your block and add 1½″ (3.8cm).

2. Cut 2 starter blocks from contrasting fabric to the desired size. *Fig. A*

3. Layer the main color (MC) with the contrasting color (CC). *Fig. B*

4. Make 2 wonky cuts in the same-ish direction. *Fig. C*

5. Switch layers so the MC and the CC alternate. *Fig. D*

6. Sew and press the seams in one direction.

7. Layer 2 sewn blocks, matching up the seam lines. *Fig. E*

8. Make two wonky cuts in the same-ish direction across the seam lines. *Fig. F*

9. Switch layers, creating a checkerboard. *Fig. G*

10. Sew and press the seams in one direction. *Fig. H*

11. Square up edges with a template or quilting ruler. One Wonky Nine-Patch is complete!

> ### TIP • Control the Wonk!
> Be mindful that the angle of your cuts isn't too shallow or too deep. You are looking for those in-between angles that are just right. Yes, we know that's the wrong story, but you get the drift. We have found that a ⅛″ (3mm) seam allowance gives the best results when sewing these wonky pieces together.

> ### TIP • Line 'em up
> When assembling the pieces, it is important to remember to line up the joins, **not** the ends of the pieces. This will ensure a cleaner finished block once those uneven outside edges are trimmed off.

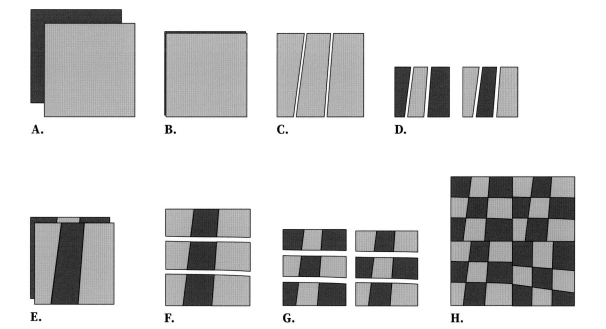

A. B. C. D.

E. F. G. H.

Oh, My Stars!

With origins ranging from Marlowe and Dickens to Beast, this celestial-based exclamation has entered into the vernacular of aunties and those who wish to temper their words around certain audiences. Growing up, we both remember this exclamation (and others), and we also both remember star blocks. One of us being from Wyoming and the other from Ohio means that our ideas of *the* star block differed, but this star block is the one that won our scrappy wonky hearts.

The Oh, My Stars! block is a compound block made up of nine component blocks, making it a Nine-Patch block. Further, it is a square-cut Nine-Patch block, so it follows the steps outlined in the Four-Patch and Nine-Patch Blocks section (page 28). The Oh, My Stars! block is featured in *The Full Monty* quilt (page 112) and is the star (see what we did there?) of the *Star Stuff* wall hanging (page 106).

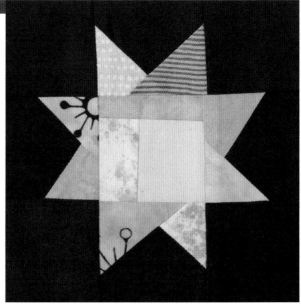

MATERIALS

8 squares of background fabric to contrast with the star

1 square to be the center of the star

Various scraps and strips for the star

CUTTING

Various widths of scraps for the center and "arms" of the "star"

8 squares of solid background fabric in your chosen size

1 square of solid star fabric in your chosen size

CONSTRUCTION

All seam allowances are ¼″ (6mm) unless otherwise noted.

The calculation for the sizes of a square-cut Nine-Patch (see Nine-Patch Calculations, page 29) apply to this block, and the general rule is also true: Divide the total width of the finished block by the number of component blocks that will make it up, then add ½″ (1.2cm) seam allowance to each of those blocks. In addition, as with all square-cut Nine-Patch blocks, Oh, My Stars! should be made in finished sizes that are divisible by 3, such as 3″, 6″, 9″, or 12″ (7.6cm, 15.2cm, 22.9cm, 30.5cm). It is possible to make blocks of other sizes, especially if they are smaller blocks that are then framed to a larger size (see Squaring Up and Framing, page 31) or included in a combo block (see Framing Combo Blocks, page 34).

Especially when piecing smaller blocks, such as for the *Star Stuff* wall hanging (page 106), be sure to place the fabric piece no higher than halfway up the side of the block, or you will cut off the tip of the point when assembling the pieces into the final block.

1. Cut 8 squares of the background fabric and 1 main color fabric in your required size.

2. Set aside 4 background squares and the square that will be the center of the star. *Fig. A*

3. First, from the remaining blocks, select a block of background fabric (Piece 1) and starting with the left or right leaning side (your choice), place a scrap of fabric (Piece 2) that covers the bottom corner of Piece 1 but extends no higher than ¼″ (6mm) from the top of Piece 1—otherwise, the tip of the star point will be eaten up by the seam allowance during assembly. Rather than measuring, estimate the height by visually looking for a point about one-third the way down from the top corner of Piece 1. Adjust the steepness of the angle as you like … this is part of the fun for this block! *Fig. B*

Roughly ⅓

4. With right sides together, sew the first star point (Piece 1) into place.

5. Press the seam to one side without trimming the excess fabric of Piece 1.

6. Now, place the sewn piece right side up. Trim any excess Piece 2 fabric, using the block shape of Piece 1 as a guide. First arm is made! *Fig. C*

7. Fold Piece 2 back along the sewn seam and trim the excess Piece 1 fabric. *Fig. D*

8. Repeat Steps 3–7 with Piece 3 (the second star point), this time leaning the fabric in the opposite direction across Piece 1 and just covering the bottom of Piece 1. The second "arm" will lay in front of the first one, so keep that in mind as you build each side of your Oh, My Stars! block. Play with various colors and which side is on top. First block of 2 star points is created! *Fig. E*

9. Repeat Steps 3–8 until you have a total of 4 star point blocks.

10. Assembling the star:

   A. Play with your final layout, adjusting on which side of the center start block each star point block will reside. *Fig. F*

   B. Assemble the block, being mindful(ish) of where corners meet (see Pressing Matters, page 19).

11. When you are ready, use a quilting ruler or square template to trim your square. Then, make more … lots more! (Or as many as required for the project.) *Fig. G*

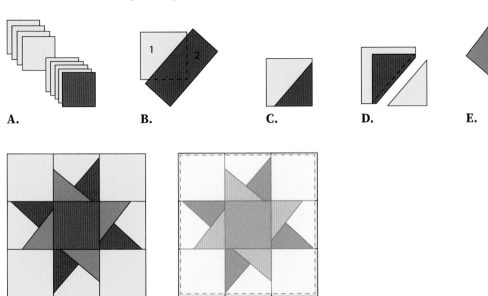

A.

B.

C.

D.

E.

F.

G.

PUTTING IT TOGETHER

The first step in putting together most of these projects is the layout of the blocks. This all-important part of the process gives you the first peek at how the finished project will look. Especially with quilts like *What She Found* (page 124) and *The Full Monty* (page 112), seeing the arrangement of blocks ahead of time is as much a part of the design process as making the blocks. For *Place* (page 115), *Upson Downs* (page 121), *She Knows* (page 118), and *Feywild* (page 136), checking that colors work together without creating hot spots and low points is important for creating a final project you are happy with.

If you are fortunate enough to have a large empty wall in your house that can serve as a design wall, that's fantastic! If, like us, your wall space is mostly taken up by shelves of books, plants, shoes … yes,

Shannon's shoes ... then you might need to be more creative. We like to use two flannel sheets pinned to the wall above the closets in our bedroom. The flannel sheets are easy to put up quickly with pins, and the blocks cling to the flannel. This gives us a big-picture look at the project and allows us to easily rearrange blocks for color play and overall composition. If there are color hot spots or low points, we simply lift off the blocks and exchange them with another block. Once we have what we think is the final layout, we use our mobile devices to gain some perspective.

Perspective

Once we have what we believe is the final layout of our piece on our design wall, we use our iPhone or iPad to take a photo. This photo gives us a forced perspective of distance, and we can take in the whole quilt in one glance. Every time we move a block, we delete the previous photo and take another one. Once we reach a **final** decision, we take one more photo and use it as a reference when we are assembling the rows to make sure we haven't mixed anything up.

This perspective works not only for final projects but for individual blocks. We find it is easy to go "block blind" while making multiples of the same block. After a while, we can lose a bit of our sensitivity to shape and design. The solution is to lay the blocks in question on a white surface and take a photo with our mobile device, prop up the device, and then step back a bit and take it in. This trick has been invaluable for us when we are making combo blocks to see how the proposed layout of the two blocks looks under a square quilting ruler (see Framing Combo Blocks, page 34).

For any instance where a little mental or physical perspective is required, a quick pic on our mobile devices does the trick.

Assembly

We like to assemble our projects in sets of two blocks, then assemble those into sets of four blocks, and then assemble the sets of four into full rows. We find this method of assembly to be cleaner overall because we can match corners more easily over shorter seams. This way, we only have a few long rows needing matched up corners.

This type of assembly works as follows:

1. Lay out the blocks for Rows 1 and 2. *Fig. A*

2. With right sides facing, sew Blocks 1 and 2 of Row 1 together and press the seams to one side.

3. Repeat Step 2 for each set of 2 blocks for the remainder of Row 1. If there is an odd number of blocks in the row, the last block will be sewn to the last set of 2, making it a set of 3. *Fig. B*

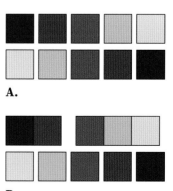

A.

B.

4. Repeat Steps 2–3 for Row 2, pressing the seams in the opposite direction. *Fig. C*

5. With right sides facing and being mindful to match up the center seams (see Nesting, page 20), attach Blocks 1/2 from Rows 1 and 2, making a set of 4 blocks. *Fig. D*

6. Press the seams to one side.

7. Repeat for all sets from Rows 1 and 2, making groups of 4. If there is an odd number of blocks in a row, the last blocks will make a group of 6. *Fig. E*

8. Sew block sets of 4 (and 6 if there is an odd number of blocks in the rows) together until Rows 1 and 2 are fully connected. *Fig. F*

9. Repeat this process, assembling 2 rows at a time. If there is an odd number of rows, the last row will remain a single row of blocks. *Fig. G*

10. Lay out the assembled row sets in the order they will be sewn together.

11. With right sides facing, pin or use Wonder Clips by Clover to secure the row sets together, being careful to match up the seams (see Nesting, page 20).

12. Sew the row sets together.

13. Continue in this manner until the quilt top is assembled. *Fig. H*

14. Give the quilt top a light press, making sure that all the seams are laying beautifully flat and even.

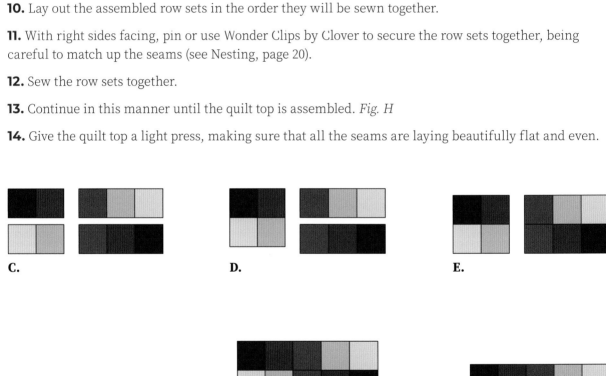

C.   **D.**   **E.**

F.

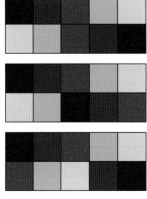

G.

H.

SETTING BOUNDARIES

Sashing and borders are design elements that folx may or may not choose to include in their projects, depending on the individual tastes of the maker. Sometimes, an appropriate sashing or border is an enhancement, but at other times, it's an unnecessary distraction.

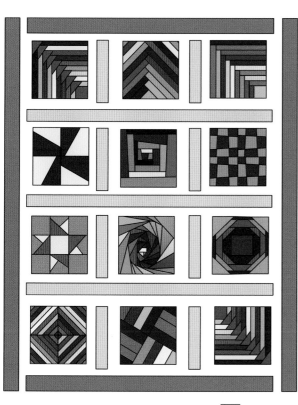

Quilt assembly

☐ Sashing
■ Border

Sashing

Sashing is a design element that consists of fabric strips placed between quilt blocks. The result is a windowpane effect that gives the eye a place to rest in the midst of a collection of visually busy scrappy wonky blocks. Again, this is a design element, and the width and color are entirely dependent on the tastes of the maker and what is appropriate for the project at hand.

The deep color of the sashing in *The Full Monty* (page 112) quilt gives the eyes a place to rest and brings out the vibrant liveliness of the individual blocks.

Not all quilts require sashing. The lack of sashing in *What She Found* (page 124) is intended to accentuate the deranged vibe of Carroll's world.

The thin pieces of blue separating the long panels of the *Upson Downs* quilt (page 121) are sashing on a large scale. The long, thin sashing strips delineate the vertical panels, giving them greater definition and accentuating the lengthwise perspective of the finished quilt.

The basic operation for sashing is as simple as it appears; sewing short strips the same length as the quilt blocks between blocks in a row. Each row is then separated by a strip the full length of that row.

1. With right sides facing, sew 1 block to 1 short strip of sashing, matching up on the right side. Follow by sewing another block to the right side of that sashing piece. Continue for each row. Press the seams in one direction for the entire row. Repeat the process for the next row, pressing seams in the opposite direction.

2. Once the rows are assembled, in the same manner, sew a sashing strip to the top of Row 1 (assuming that sashing is used there). Follow by sewing a sashing strip to the bottom of Row 1. Sew the top of Row 2 to the bottom of the first assembled strip. Continue until the quilt is assembled.

Border

The *border* is fabric that encompasses the assembled blocks (with or without sashing) and is part of the actual quilt top. Like sashing, the border gives the eye a resting place and also enhances the look of the overall quilt in the same way that a good picture frame complements the subject of the photo. Once again, the border is a design element, and the width and color are dependent on the aesthetics of the maker and what is appropriate for each project.

We continued the lengthening perspective of *Upson Downs* (page 121) with a border of the same blue fabric as the sashing strips.

The Full Monty quilt (page 112) benefits from a border and sashing to enhance the scrappy wonky block. In fact, this quilt has a double border. We couldn't settle on just a solid colored border, so we added the scrappy wonky pieced border with keystone blocks at the corners. What can we say? We just couldn't get enough of a wonky good thing.

Border or binding? In the case of *What She Found* (page 124), we decided that the quilt, like a chess board, needed a border. We opted to use a narrow binding that, in effect, gave the quilt a border without adding an actual border to the quilt top.

Borders are assembled by adding strips of fabric to two of the sides of the quilt top, which is then capped off by strips going across the top and bottom ends.

It is easy to jumble up the terminology for all the fabric that goes around quilt blocks and quilt tops. In short, *framing* expands a block to a trimmed size, *sashing* refers to strips placed between blocks, and a *border* is fabric that goes around the assembled blocks and becomes the outer edges of the final quilt top. Binding, facing, and bagging are finishing techniques that cover the raw edges of, and join, the layers of the quilt sandwich and create a fully enclosed edge. We talk about those in Livin' on the Edge (page 82).

VISUALIZE THE OUTCOME

Jason works daily with graphics programs, so we take advantage of his skills to visualize different sashing and border options. He lays out photos of the blocks in the arrangement they will be in the finished project and then changes the border and sashing options for width and color. Okay ... so a lot of that process is really Shannon standing behind his chair, asking for endless changes ... but it works well for us.

If those particular electronic skills are not in your wheelhouse, no worries! Lay out a good-sized piece of fabric (enough to lay out several blocks at least) in the color or colors you are thinking of using and arrange your quilt blocks on the fabric. This method gives you a solid visual for your final project. We have done this for framing, sashing, and borders when we needed a physical representation rather than a virtual one. We also use our mobile device to gain a distance perspective on the potential design (see Perspective, page 69).

THE SANDWICH: TO FLUFF OR NOT TO FLUFF?

Let's talk about the sandwich. Unfortunately, we are not referencing the amazing pastrami on rye we crave from THAT deli in New York; rather, this sandwich is the layers of the quilt itself. Put simply, the layers of a quilt sandwich are the quilt top, the batting or interlining, and the backing. Taking a deeper dive into the strata, we find that a multitude of options exist to fit any climate, use, and personal taste.

Top Layer

This one is a given for a quilt project, right? But wait—not all the projects here are quilts. Now what? Let's adjust that definition a bit to say "quilt top" and describe any public-facing side of a project. This term encompasses the top of the placemats, the outside of the vest, the outside of the bag, and so forth. All the projects in this book are assembled with a sandwich, and that outer layer count as the top layer of the sandwich, be it a on a quilt or a coaster.

Middle Layer

This layer provides shape, support, firmness, texture, and warmth. The right material in the middle layer combined with the right quilting pattern adds density, stability, and firmness to a project and helps the overall piece maintain its shape through wear and washing. Options include batting, interfacing, and stabilizer, depending on the outcome you wish to achieve.

Function, the end result you seek for your project to be used as intended, is key when choosing the product to use in this middle layer. Viable options include batting, muslin, a sheet, old shirts sewn together into a solid piece of fabric, fusible interfacing, insulated hot/cold interfacing, a shower curtain (wait for it …), and even old quilts. Everything depends on the project.

Batting

Batting comes in a variety of thicknesses and materials to encompass a wide range of project possibilities. We love the Hobbs Tuscany Collection Silk Batting for our garments and for our lighter-weight quilts, when we want added stability, just a little warmth, and a low-profile quilting detail. The same goes for the Hobbs Thermore batting, which was originally designed for garments. On the other hand, the Hobbs Poly-Down and Heirloom Premium Wool have more loft (they are thicker), so the quilting creates a higher profile texture (more of that lovely "quilty," puffy feel). In thicker batting, the benefit of added air circulation due to the looser fibers means that the quilts will provide greater warmth without turning you into a sweaty mess in the middle of the night.

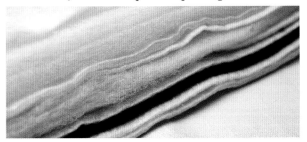

Our friends at Hobbs Batting provided us with a variety of sizes and thicknesses of batting for the projects in this book.

Interfacing and Stabilizers

Interfacing and stabilizers are another option for the middle layer of projects when you want to add stability without bulk. Both come in a variety of weights and can be ironed on to the back or between fabrics, adding stability to such projects as the cuffs and collar of the *Rose Tattoo* (page 127) and home decor items, such as totes, coasters, and placemats.

Alternative Options

Sometimes, we don't use typical materials for the middle layer in our projects. We both grew up with quilts that had cotton or flannel sheets, sewn-together cotton shirts, and even other quilts as the middle layer. We have used flannel and cotton sheets and muslin left over from our garment projects as a middle layer, depending on the effect we were looking for and, frankly, the materials we had available at the time. Also, we are hot sleepers and enjoy summer quilts (more on that in a minute) with no interfacing or a thin layer of lightweight cotton fabric (that is, a sheet) as the middle layer. This option gives added weight and stability to the quilt without the unwanted warmth of a heavier quilt.

Oh yeah … back to the shower curtains. Want a picnic blanket that will prevent your perfect repast from ending in a soggy bottom? Use a plastic or vinyl shower curtain or liner or even a vinyl tablecloth as your interfacing! Sewing and quilting through this material can be achieved with a regular home machine, heavy-duty thread, and a jeans or other heavy-duty needle.

Speaking of picnics, a product like Insul-Fleece™ from C&T Publishing is a metalized mylar insulated interfacing that will turn your *Totes Cute Tote* into an insulated hot/cold carrier. It is also the perfect choice to turn coasters and placemats into trivets, giving added protection to your surfaces.

Come to the Dark Side

Colors? Yes. Light and dark. Why use a dark batting? Imagine having a top made in a gorgeously dark color palette and then adding white batting. That white batting is going to shine through and break your deep vibe. Same goes for the opposite scenario with black batting and a light-colored top, as seen on *Place* (page 115). Not a great pairing, as the dark batting will make the light fabric appear dingy. Thankfully, you have choices. You might need to look a bit further for dark batting, but it's out there, and it's worth the search to ensure that your project is just that much more perfectly finished.

Bottom Layer

The back of quilts, and of most projects where the top is the highlight, is often an afterthought. Backings are the unsung heroes of the quilting world. We get it. Everyone wants to focus on the pretty, pieced, wonky goodness. We don't blame y'all one bit. However, a good backing means stability, and for quilts and garments, it is the layer that is going to be next to your skin. For coasters and

placemats, it is the final layer of protection for your furniture. In addition, imagine being finished with your wonky creation and ready to move forward with the finishing, but *noooooo* … you have to make decisions about the backing and maybe even order the backing in the color you want. So, now you wait. Preplanning your bottom layer is an important step in the creative process and should not be overlooked.

As with the middle layer, function plays a huge part in the decision about which type of backing to use. What is your project, and how will you use it? Answer that, and you are on your way. Pieced backing can be made from any fabric, including denim, old work shirts, and regular quilting cotton, and can be as beautiful as the top, making your finished piece a reversible work of art.

The other option to seek is wide backs, or wides. All the large quilts in this book (and most of our personal quilts) are backed with wides from Robert Kaufman Fabrics. We mostly prefer a soft white backing for our quilts, and our go-to is Robert Kaufman Fabrics, Kona Wide, color Bone K082–1037 (yes, we have that description in our quick-paste clipboard because we use it just that often). We don't have to worry about piecing and pattern matching, and Kona Wide comes in a range of colors, so colored and darker quilt tops can be paired with a coordinating colored or darker backing to complete the overall vibe. We even found a luxurious red plaid flannel wide fabric from Robert Kaufman Fabrics that was the perfect backing for *She Knows* (page 118).

Whether you choose pieced, wide back, cotton, flannel, or denim, don't be afraid to embrace your creative chaos a bit and have fun with your quilt backs.

Summer Quilts

Okay, let's talk about the big exception to the rule: summer quilts. If you grew up in parts of the world where the climate is regularly more hot than cold, you are probably familiar with summer quilts, whether you know it or not. If you ever sat outside or on a screened-in porch on a summer evening or fall day, and a chill started to set in, but you were fine because you had grabbed that quilt draped over the back of the seat and wrapped up in it, you probably used a summer quilt. Both of us grew up with these types of quilts. What makes it a summer quilt? Summer quilts are lightweight and usually made with only two layers: a top and a backing. That said, we definitely had quilts called summer quilts that also had an inner layer made from old cotton sheets. We have used cotton sheets and muslin in our summer quilts. Don't let the name fool you into thinking that these perfectly weighted quilts are only for the summer months. We have at least one summer quilt on our bed year-round and at least two near the couch for sitting under on those chilly nights when we don't want to turn on the

The Lotus Pond Throw from *Boro & Sashiko, Harmonious Imperfection* was constructed in summer-quilt fashion, with just two layers.

heaters or we're only a little cool. Those are the times when a summer quilt with no middle layer or a very light fabric middle layer comes in handy. And, if you happen to have a summer porch to sit on as the light fades and you just aren't ready to go in yet, this is the quilt to reach for.

Basting

Basting is the act of taking the layers of your sandwich and tacking them together so you can sew through the layers without them shifting. The trick here is taking care that all the layers are smooth and free of wrinkles as you go. Wrinkles will make your finished quilt end up lumpy after quilting, and we definitely don't want that!

We recommend spray-basting your quilts, as it is fast and simple and ensures that your layers stay together as you sew. The downside is that aerosol-spray baste can be a little messy and expensive. If this is an issue for you, pin-basting is your new best friend.

Spray Basting

1. Make sure that the backing and middle layers are at least 2″ (5cm) wider than your top on all sides. If you are sending your quilt out to be quilted, you will need them to be at least 4″ (10cm) wider.

2. On a clean flat surface, spread out the backing, right side down. Smooth it carefully and tape the edges to the surface. Regardless of whether you are working on wood floors, carpet, or the concrete in your garage, painter's tape will hold the backing flat and wrinkle-free while you spray and spread the upcoming layers.

3. Place your batting down on top of the quilt back, taking care to set it straight and smooth it out before you begin to spray.

4. Fold up one edge about 24″ (61cm) and spray the backing with a light amount of spray baste.

5. Lay the batting back down, again smoothing to keep any wrinkles at bay.

6. Roll the opposite side of the batting down to the sprayed section.

7. Spraying a small section of the exposed back at a time, smooth the batting into place, rolling as you go.

8. Repeat this process with the quilt top.

Pin Basting

1. Make sure that the backing and middle layers are at least 2″ (5cm) wider on all sides than your top. If you are sending your quilt out to be quilted, you will need them to be at least 4″ (10cm) wider.

2. On a clean flat surface, spread out the backing, right side down. Smooth it carefully and tape the edges to the surface, keeping it lightly taut. Regardless of whether you are working on wood floors, carpet, or concrete, painter's tape will help hold the backing flat and wrinkle-free while you spread and pin the upcoming layers.

3. Place the batting on top of the quilt back, again taking care to set it straight and smooth it carefully.

4. Repeat this process with the quilt top.

5. Starting from the center of the quilt and moving outward, use coilless safety pins to pin through all 3 layers. Pin every few inches, smoothing as you go.

6. Keep pinning.

7. Tired yet? Keep pinning …

8. After pinning, flip the sandwich over and check for wrinkles, pleats, or serious puckers. If you spot any, sigh, swear a little, take a deep breath, and either begin again or look for a way to smooth them out by removing a few pins at a time and working the wrinkle off the edge.

GETTIN' STITCHY WITH IT

Quilting

Now, we come to the most entangled discussion in the life of those who sew quilty projects: the quilting. Wait … this is called a quilt, and what we are doing is called quilting, and when we are making a quilt we are quilters, and the stitches that bind the layers of a quilt together are called the quilting? *Schoolhouse Rock* didn't cover this situation in the person, place, or thing song. Without delving into the properties of transitive and intransitive verbs, let's speak **briefly** about the act of sewing the layers of our creations together: quilting (transitive verb, in case you were curious).

Everyone has their personal preference for quilting their projects. Shannon grew up sitting at a large quilting frame with small lamps set in the middle of the suspended quilt, listening to her grandmother and great-aunts chat. Jason grew up with a domestic machine quilter who would, occasionally, send her quilts out to a longarm quilter. All quilting styles are valid, and we encourage everyone to explore, experiment, and, yes, follow their creative chaos to find what they love and do

what works for their projects. What we will say is this: Practice. Make a sample sandwich and play. Play with thread weights, designs, straight-stitch lines and free-motion quilting, machine, and hand stitching. Practice with plain fabric tops and with pieced tops.

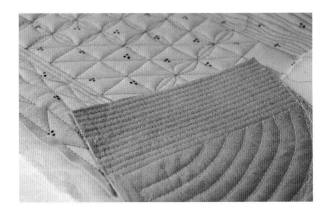

We make a practice sandwich from a square of plain fabric as the top for new patterns and designs we have not used before. The plain fabric allows us to see the stitches more easily, and then we can decide which, if any, will make it to our final projects.

For pieced practice sandwiches, we have a healthy stack of blocks that just didn't work out, weren't exactly the color scheme we were looking for, or simply didn't make their way into projects for this book. After sewing a few of those together to create a small quilt top for use in a sandwich, we test the proposed stitch pattern for the larger quilt, making sure that it isn't going to distract from or break up the scrappy wonky beauty of our blocks.

Bonus: Both of these sandwiches are valuable for practicing your binding, bagging, or facing (see Livin' on the Edge, page 82) if you haven't done that before. Ours usually end up being mug rugs in the studio or left out on the back patio. Just a thought.

The one underlying objective we keep in mind when picking the quilt patterns for our projects (in case you missed this sentence before) is to ensure that the quilting will not distract from or break up the scrappy wonky vibe of our blocks. We love more complex quilting designs, but when we stitch them on a practice sandwich of the quilt or project we are making, some of them are just too much, and they overwhelm the blocks. So, we take a photo, make a note, and save the idea for later.

READY TO START

Here are a few tips for when you are ready to start quilting:

1. Lengthen your stitches a bit. Because you are stitching through layers of fabric, you need a slightly longer stitch. How long? That depends on your sandwich. Start with 2.5–3.0mm (8–10 stitches per inch) and go from there. A practice sandwich will tell you everything you need to know.

2. Use a walking foot or dual-feed mechanism. A walking foot is the perfect tool for quilting. It ensures that the quilt sandwich is pulled by the machine feed dogs below and the foot above. This keeps the fabric straight and eliminates wrinkles that can happen when you're using only a regular sewing foot. If your machine has a dual-feed mechanism like the one found in our BERNINA 790 Plus and BERNINA 570QE, you can use that in lieu of the walking foot. It's not exactly the same but will still give you beautiful results.

3. Slow down! If your machine has a speed dial or slider, lower it. You are not in a race. Take your time and enjoy the methodical process.

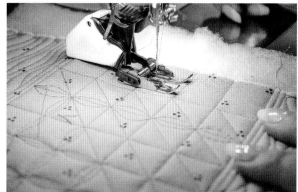

4. Start at the center and work out. To keep your quilt from skewing as you sew, start from the center and work out to the edges.

5. Quilt every other line. Along with Tip 4, quilting every other line and then going back to fill in ensures that your quilt stays flat and even.

READY TO PRACTICE? HERE ARE A FEW EXAMPLES TO START WITH

Stitch-in-the-Ditch

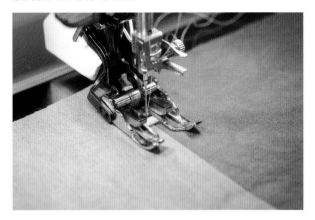

Outline

Stitch-in-the-ditch is a stylistically simple and clean way to quilt your projects. Simply place your needle in the "ditch" where the blocks are joined and follow that line. Sandwich secured. No lines or designs to distract from your wonkiness.

Outline quilting is the cousin of stitch-in-the-ditch, as it can follow that same ditch as a guide or follow the shapes of the pieces in your quilt blocks. Unlike stitch-in-the-ditch, outline quilting is visible, and the stitching line can be as close to the sewn seams as you like or farther away.

Lines

Straight- and wavy-line quilting is one of our favorite forms of stitching for our scrappy wonky projects because it creates those lovely crinkles that result from the fabric raising up between the stitched lines. Lines, whether straight or wavy, can be as close together or far apart as you need and can be varied in distance from one another for a beautiful texture. The most important part of this style of quilting is that the stitching lines run in one direction, even if that direction meanders a bit. Wonky lines! We definitely recommend exploring the different styles for yourself.

Grids

Grids take straight-line quilting to the next level. Instead of lines running in one direction, stitch lines running in two directions to create a grid. Square grids, 30°-angle grids, and wavy-line grids are favorites of ours. This style of quilting creates clean, structural, gorgeous lines that can be as close together or far apart as is appropriate for your projects and is not so busy as to break up the wonkiness.

Sashiko

WOAH! What was that? Sashiko? Given our past, you didn't think that we would pass up the most obvious of hand-quilting techniques in our repertoire, did you? For those who are not aware, our previous two books are about different forms of sashiko hand stitching. The first of those books, *Boro & Sashiko, Harmonious Imperfection*, is specifically about hitomezashi and moyouzashi sashiko, which are both perfect for quilting. So, yes, we use that style of sashiko to hand stitch some of the projects in this book. If you already have a copy of that book, *fab* and thank you! If not, go grab a copy from our website or our publisher's website ... it's okay ... we'll wait here. Got it? Good. And thank you! Now, go find a

stitch pattern that you really love and learn it. If you have already done sashiko with us before, make a practice sandwich and familiarize yourself with stitching through that type of medium. Our preferred style of sashiko for our quilty projects is classical and modern moyouzashi and hitomezashi, as seen in the *Dinner with Friends* placemats (page 92) and the *Star Stuff* wall hanging (page 106).

Whatever style of quilting is employed in a given project, check with the batting manufacturer to see how close together or far apart they recommend that quilting lines be when you're using different weights of batting. Hobbs Batting has a lovely chart on its website that lists all of that information for its batting products. You might also need to experiment with stitch length, depending on the thickness of the middle layer of your projects, as shorter stitch lengths can lead to thread breakage. For hand quilting techniques like sashiko, the density and thickness of your fabric will determine how large your stitches can be and how close together your lines can be. Again ... practice!

If you want to follow our quilting path, at the beginning of each project, we list what type of quilting we did: stitch-in-the-ditch, outline, straight line, grid, sashiko, and so forth.

LIVIN' ON THE EDGE

The scraps have all been wonked, the sandwich has been assembled, the layers have been quilted together, and now you are ready to crown your creation with the perfect finish to bring it all together. Binding, framing, and bagging are finishing techniques that join the layers of the quilt sandwich and encase the raw edges of the quilt.

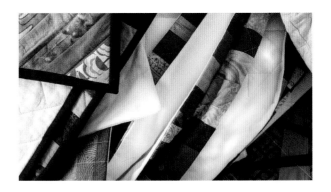

Binding

Binding enfolds the raw edges of the layers of the quilt sandwich and provides a visible border around the quilt top. The width of this binding border can vary according to how much of a border you want to show around the edge of your quilt. The binding as border is a great alternative to adding an actual border to the quilt top. The binding is another step that is often an afterthought but should be decided upon as soon as the color scheme of the finished quilt is apparent. This way, the fabric needed to create the binding strips can be purchased in advance, and the binding is ready to go when the quilting is finished.

Narrow vs. Wide

Binding is only as wide as the batting and backing beyond the edge of the quilt top. When trimming the batting and backing of the quilt after adding quilting lines, include the width of the binding in the trimming. For example, leave 1″, 2″ (2.5cm, 5cm), and so forth of batting and backing around the edge of the quilt, depending on how wide the binding is to be. In *She Knows* (page 118) and *What She Found* (page 124), we wanted a ¼″ (6mm) binding, so no additional trim was needed because there was already a ¼″ (6mm) seam allowance in the quilt.

Binding Width Quick Reference Formula

To create binding of any width for any project, here is a quick reference formula for you to follow:

Desired binding width x 4 + ½″ (1.2cm) seam allowance + approximately ¼″ (6mm) extra for folding over and batting thickness = binding width to cut.

For example:

2″ (5cm) desired binding width x 4 = 8″ (20.3cm) + ½″ (1.2cm) seam allowance = 8½″ (21.6cm) + ¼″ (6mm) extra = 8¾″ (22.2cm) binding width to cut.

General Instructions

Regardless of the size of your binding, here are general instructions to follow for binding your projects. The measurements for these instructions are what we used for our ¼″ bindings. If you want a wider binding, adjust accordingly.

1. Trim the edges of the quilt, using a straight edge.

2. Create binding strips, joining to make longer strips as needed, or use bias tape that is at least 2½″ (6.4cm) wide. Fold it in half lengthwise with wrong sides together and press.

3. With the quilt facing right side up, beginning in the center of one side, lay the raw edge of the folded binding strip flush with the raw edge of the quilt, allowing 10″ (25cm) of extra binding unstitched as you begin.

4. Sew the binding with a ¼″ (6mm) seam allowance.

5. Sew the binding until you get close to a corner. When you are ¼″ (6mm) from the corner, leave your needle down and rotate the quilt under the needle. Stitch a short diagonal line toward the corner of the quilt. Lift the needle and cut the thread.

6. Rotate the quilt 90° and flip the binding straight up so that it is at a 90° angle from the binding you just stitched.

7. Fold the binding over the flipped fabric and continue flush with the next side of the quilt top. This will create a mitered corner when you turn the binding to the back.

8. Again, stitch ¼″ (6mm) from the edge of the sandwich along the next side. Repeat each corner in the same manner.

9. Stop sewing about 10″ (25cm) from your starting point. Overlap the starting point by the width of the binding, trimming away the excess.

10. Open both pieces of the binding and turn the binding that's below the overlap right side up at a 90° angle to the edge of the quilt. Turn the binding that is on top of the overlap right side down and match the corners and edges of both pieces.

11. Stitch the overlapped binding at a 45° angle from the upper left corner of the overlap to the bottom of the lower right corner.

12. Trim the corner off, leaving ¼″ (6mm) seam allowance.

13. Fold and complete machine sewing the binding.

14. Turn the binding to the back side and use Wonder Clips by Clover to hold it in place.

15. Machine or hand sew the back of the binding (See Ladder Stitch, page 23).

Facing

A facing works similar to a binding, with the exception that no fabric shows on the front side of the quilt. We love facing our quilts and wall hangings when we want a clean, unbroken edge. The front of the quilt "floats," with no line around the edge to break the visual impact of the design.

We opted to use a facing for the *Place* quilt (page 115) to preserve the clean, floating look of the individual blocks.

1. Trim the edges of the quilt to square them up.

2. If you are making a project that will be hung, cut 4 squares that are each 4″ × 4″ (10 × 10cm) for the corners. Fold each in half, making a triangle, and press. If you are not hanging your project with corner squares, skip this step. *Fig. A*

3. Cut 2 strips for the top and bottom that are 3″–4″ (8–10cm) wide and the same length as the quilt's width. Fold each in half lengthwise, wrong sides together, and press.

4. Cut 2 strips for the left and right sides that are 3″–4″ (8–10cm) wide and as long as the quilt is long. Fold each in half lengthwise, wrong sides together, and press.

5. If you're using hanging corners, with the quilt right side up, place the corners on top of the quilt. *Fig. B*

6. Lay the facing strips along the short sides and then on the long sides (on top of the triangles, if using), with *cut sides along the quilt edge*. NOTE: DO NOT place the folded edge along the quilt edge.

7. If you're using hanging corners, trim the border strips so they begin and end roughly at the center of each corner triangle; they should not go all the way to the end. *Fig. C*

A: Facing 1
Cut 2.
4″ (10cm) wide
Width of the quilt

B: Facing 2
Cut 2.
4″ (10cm) wide
Length of the quilt

C: Corners
Cut 4 squares 4″ (10cm).
Fold in half.

Q: Quilt sandwich
Right side up

A.

B.

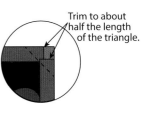

Trim to about half the length of the triangle.

C.

8. Sew a ¼″ (6mm) seam around the entire quilt. Make sure that you are sewing through all layers. *Fig. D*

9. Trim off the dog ears just to the stitch line and turn everything to the back of the quilt.

10. Press the facing flat and turn it to the back of the quilt. Hand stitch the facing strips to the quilt back by using the appliqué stitch, catching a few threads from the strip and the backing fabric. *Fig. E*

By including the corner pieces, you can use a dowel rod or curtain rod inserted into the corners running across the edge to hang your quilt!

D.

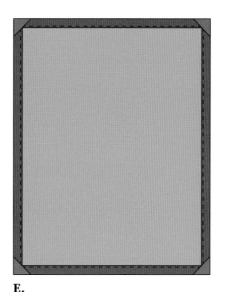

E.

Bagging

Bagging provides a clean, undisturbed edge to your pieces without the use of binding or facing. Think of bagging as making a pillow without the pillow insert. The edges of the sandwich are sewn together with the right sides of the top and backing facing one another, and then the whole affair is turned right side out. This technique can be done for a three-layer or two-layer sandwich. Unlike binding and facing, bagging is done before the quilting is done, and it is important to thread or pin baste the layers to prevent shifting during quilting.

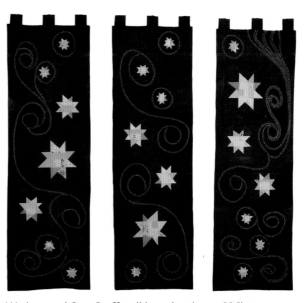

We bagged *Star Stuff* wall hanging (page 106) to preserve the edges with no visible border, but also to keep the thickness of the edges to a minimum.

1. Trim the edges of the quilt.

2. Layer the sandwich. *Fig. A*

Be very careful how you layer your sandwich when using 3 layers, or you could end up with the wrong order when you turn the quilt right side out. The layers should be (from bottom to top): batting or lining, quilt top, backing fabric laid face down on the quilt top.

3. Pin the edges of the quilt sandwich to prevent shifting during sewing. *Fig. B*

4. Sew around the edges of the sandwich, leaving roughly one-third of a short side open for ease of turning. *Fig. C*

5. Trim the corners to, but not through, the sewn line and turn the sandwich. To make sure that all the corners are nicely pointed, we use a point turner or the corner of a ruler.

6. Use the ladder stitch (page 23) to close the opening left for turning. *Fig. D*

7. Lay the quilt on a flat surface and smooth out the layers so they are even.

8. Beginning with the center and working outward, pin baste the layers together.

9. Quilt as desired.

A.

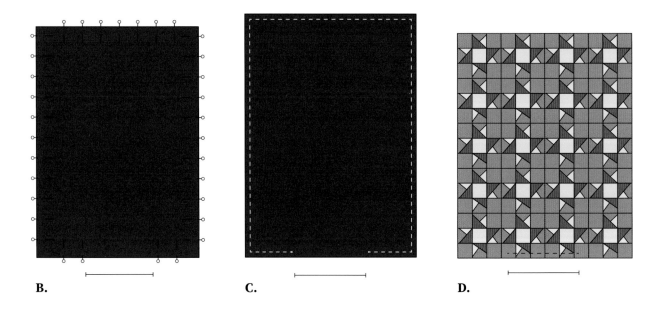

B.　　　　　　　　　**C.**　　　　　　　　　**D.**

JUST HANGING AROUND

Even if your quilt isn't initially intended to be hung gallery-style in the hallowed halls of your home, having a means of doing so is a great option, just in case you decide that all of your labors deserve a viewing other than when you are donning your sleeping cap for the night. And what if someone is coming over who you just know **needs** to marvel at your creation? A means to hang your projects is a good option to have. Besides, they look really cool, so why hide them?

If you wish to display your quilt on a wall, you can add a rod pocket for ease of display.

Pocket Instructions

Cut 1 piece of fabric 9″ (23cm) wide x the same length as the side of your quilt where you are attaching the pocket.

1. With the right side down, fold the side edges in ¼″ (6mm) and press.

2. Fold again ½″ (1.2cm) and press.

3. Sew the folded edge down to secure.

4. Fold the panel in half lengthwise with the wrong sides facing each other. Pin or clip and sew using a ½″ (1.2cm) seam allowance. Press the seam open.

5. Press flat with the seam centered on what will be the back of the rod pocket.

6. With the rod pocket oriented horizontally, pull the top layer of fabric down, moving the pressed top fold line ½″ (1.2cm) toward the center. Press a new fold line. This will create a bubble of fabric that will allow the hanging rod to be inserted without distorting the front of the piece.

7. Measure 1″ (2.5cm) down from the edge of the quilt and hand sew the rod pocket in place using whip stitches, appliqué stitches, or ladder stitches along the top and bottom pressed edges.

For large quilts, it is best to use two rod pockets with at least 6″ (15.2cm) space between them. That space allows for extra hanging support to be placed at the center of the rod.

The Projects

Like the blocks themselves, our projects are presented in order, starting with projects that require less concentration, allowing access to first-time quilters and presenting experienced quilters with fun projects they can finish relatively quickly and still use to demonstrate their new skills. Those who have never created a quilt before can start with the first projects and work their way up to making full-blown textile art pieces.

THE METHOD

Because we don't want your creativity to be limited to **just** the projects in this book, here is how to bring your own ideas to life.

1. Pick a block or blocks.

2. Pick a size (pillow, wall hanging, lap throw, quilt, coasters).

3. Pick your framing.

4. Pick a finish.

5. *Go!*

Although we do provide specific projects in this next section that use specific blocks laid out in a specific way, as well as specific border, sashing, and finishing techniques, they are not meant to be hard and fast designs. Think of them more as recipes that you can use to make your own creations. Further, the techniques for borders, sashing, finishing, and assembly are all interchangeable. If you have a block that you really love, choose that one for your layout, add sashing or not, include a border or binding, or decide that facing is what makes your creative energy soar. For example, the pieced border with keystone blocks for *The Full Monty* quilt (page 112) is a technique that could be applied to any of the quilts or wall hangings in this book.

Further, make the quilts in any size you want or expand a wall hanging to become a throw or a quilt. Again, we present them in the sizes we wanted *our* designs to be showcased in. Your tastes might be different, so don't be afraid to embrace that creative chaos and follow your instincts.

Whatever the case, use our projects as exact blueprints to follow or use them as a jumping-off point to create your own masterpiece. It's up to you, and nothing would make us happier than to see how our designs inspired you to follow your own creative chaos.

JAVA JIVE

Whether you like coffee or you like tea, coasters are a necessary item in the home to ensure that your favorite beverage doesn't leave an indelible mark on Great-Grandma's side table. Nothing says that even a functional item can't have some creative flair. Make these coasters as an immediate gratification project while you practice your new scrappy wonky block skills. They don't require a lot of time to create, and they look great on a coffee table or on the dining room table on game night. Pair these with placemats for scrappy wonky sets and make some extras for housewarming gifts. Or just keep them all yourself … that's good, too.

FINISHED COASTER: 5″ × 5″ (12.7 × 12.7cm)

MATERIALS

Large(ish) scraps of denim fabric (Time to cut into those jeans that may or may not fit again someday … just us?)

Scraps for a chosen quilt block

CUTTING

Cut 6 squares 5½″ × 5½″ (14 × 14cm) of denim

CONSTRUCTION

All seams are sewn at ¼″ (6mm) unless otherwise noted.

Blocks

Make 6 scrappy wonky quilt blocks of your choice that are each 5½″ × 5½″ (14 × 14cm) square. We used Fly Away Home, Drunken Pineapple, Steppin' Up, All-Seeing Eye, Love Shack, and Scrappy Wonky Rose. Use your favorite(s).

Assemble the Coasters

1. Pin or clip the top and back together, right sides facing, and sew ¼″ (6mm) around the edges, leaving a 2″ (5cm) opening on 1 side for turning.

2. Trim the corners down to, without cutting through, the sewn seam.

3. Turn right side out through the opening.

4. Press flat, being sure to press the edges of the turning opening to the inside of the coaster. This ensures that the opening will be sewn closed in the next step.

5. Close the opening with an appliqué stitch or topstitch a scant ⅛″ (3mm) around all edges.

DINNER WITH FRIENDS

Count Basie set the mood for a raucous evening of dining. Whether your menu includes takeout pizza or a nine-course extravaganza, these placemats will serve as the perfect bass ... umm ... base for your evening. As a project, placemats are a step up in concentration level from coasters ... but not much of a step, so they are still an immediate gratification project. Coordinate these with your coasters for scrappy wonky sets. We tend to find ourselves making extra blocks out of sheer excitement, and coasters and placemats are the perfect use for those ideas. As we said, you could make these as sets with the coasters and give them away for housewarming gifts. Or you could keep them all for yourself and give your friends a copy of this book so they can learn to make their own. Just sayin' ...

FINISHED PLACEMAT: 18″ × 12″ (45.7 × 30.5cm)

MATERIALS

1¼ yards (1.2m) denim fabric

3–4 yards (2.8–3.7m) various scraps for piecing and framing

CUTTING

Cut 6 rectangles 18½″ × 12½″ (47 × 32cm) from denim backing fabric.

Individual placemat cuts are shown in the diagrams following.

CONSTRUCTION

All seams are sewn at ¼″ (6mm) unless otherwise noted. All top stitching is ⅛″ (3mm).

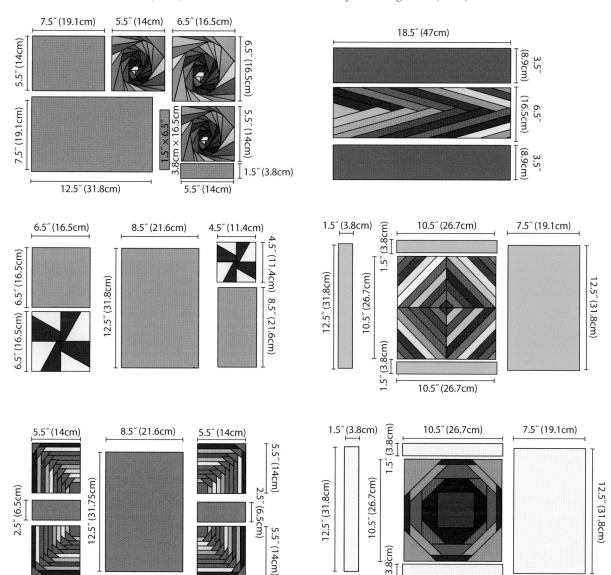

Placemat assembly

Make the Pieced Blocks

After choosing a layout from the assembly diagrams, make blocks that can be combined and/or trimmed to the required sizes. Some blocks can be made to size, while others are more easily framed and trimmed. You may choose to machine or hand quilt your placemats; we hand stitched sashiko patterns from our book *Boro & Sashiko, Harmonious Imperfection* for ours. Here are the details for our placemats and the colors we selected:

Scrappy Wonky Rose, Upper Right

- 1 block 6½″ × 6½″ (16.5 × 16.5cm)
- 2 blocks 5½″ × 5½″ (14 × 14cm)
- Sashiko stitching in Aurifil 12-weight, color #5022 and color #1147 held together
- Sashiko pattern: Linked seven treasures

Entwined panel, Center Horizontal

- 1 panel 6½″ × 18½″ (16.5 × 47cm)
- Sashiko stitching in Aurifil 12-weight, color #5006
- Sashiko pattern: Blue ocean waves

All-Seeing Eye, Left Center

- 1 block 10½″ × 10½″ (26.7 × 26.7cm)
- Sashiko stitching in Aurifil 12-weight, color #4657 and color #2395 held together
- Sashiko pattern: Mountain form variation

Fly Away Home in Each of the Four Corners

- 4 blocks 5½″ × 5½″ (14 × 14cm)
- Sashiko stitching in Aurifil 12-weight, color #1100
- Sashiko pattern: Rice stitch variation 2

Drunken Pineapple, Left Center

- 1 block 10½″ × 10½″ (26.7 × 26.7cm)

- Sashiko stitching in Aurifil 12-weight, color #1240 and color #3840 held together
- Sashiko pattern: Asanoha

Don Quixote

- 1 block in lower left corner 6½″ × 6½″ (16.5 × 16.5cm)
- 1 block in upper right corner 4½″ × 4½″ (11.4 × 11.4cm)
- Sashiko stitching in Aurifil 12-weight, color #2240 and color #1133 held together
- Sashiko pattern: Pinwheels

Assemble the Front Panels

1. Piece together the top panels to the sizes shown on the placemat assembly.

2. Press the seams away from the pieced panel.

3. Square up the fabric to 18½″ × 12½″ (47 × 32cm), using a quilting ruler or template.

Quilting

We used sashiko to hand quilt the large open spaces of the placemats. All the sashiko patterns used are in our book *Boro & Sashiko, Harmonious Imperfection.* Quilt your placemats as suits your taste.

Construct the Placemats

1. Pin or clip the layers together and sew ¼″ (6mm) around the edges, leaving a 3″ (7.6cm) opening on one side for turning.

2. Trim the corners down to, without cutting through, the sewn seam.

3. Turn right side out through the opening.

4. Press flat, being sure to press the edges of the turning opening to the inside of the placemat. This ensures that the opening will be sewn closed in the next step.

5. Close the opening with an appliqué stitch or topstitch a scant ⅛″ (3mm) around all edges.

PILLOW TALK

As far as on-screen pairs go, Rock Hudson and Doris Day were sublime. These pillows make an equally perfect pairing for the quilts and wall-hanging projects in this book, or they could avoid the drama and go solo. The most appealing feature of pillows as a project is their versatility. You can choose any block and turn it into a pillow by using any configuration that makes you happy. Use four blocks like we did with the Wonky Nine-Patch or one giant block like we did with the Scrappy Wonky Rose. Maybe you really like framed blocks like we used in the *Place* quilt (page 115). Great! Make your pillow that way. Any block and configuration combination that strikes your fancy works perfectly for these projects. That said, if you would like to try a certain block but aren't sure of how many of them you really want to make, pillows make a perfect showcase for that favorite design. Make pillows to accompany the different quilts and wall hangings to add another layer to the interior design genius that you are (we think that Doris would have approved). Our pillows are made by using a lapped-back method. This assembly allows for easy cleaning and makes it easy to switch them out, depending on the quilt or wall hanging we have on display in that room.

MATERIALS

14″ × 14″ (35.6 × 35.6cm) pillow insert, OR

18″ × 18″ (45.7 × 45.7cm) pillow insert, OR

20″ × 20″ (50.8 × 50.8cm) pillow insert (We like Hobbs Poly-Down Pillow Pals Pillow Inserts.)

½–¾ yard (46–69cm) of heavy cotton fabric or canvas

Framing/sashing fabric to fit your chosen assembly

Batting: 1 square to match pillow top (14″ × 14″ [35.6 × 35.6cm]/18″ × 18″ [45.7 × 45.7cm]/20″ × 20″ [50.8 × 50.8cm])

Thread

Machine quilting in Aurifil 50-weight, color #5010

CUTTING

For 14″ pillow: Cut 2 rectangles 13½″ × 11¼″ (34.3 × 28.6cm) back fabric

For 18″ pillow: Cut 2 rectangles 17½″ × 13¼″ (44.5 × 33.6cm) back fabric

For 20″ pillow: Cut 2 rectangles 19½″ × 15¼″ (49.5 × 38.7cm) back fabric

20″ Pillow Form

19.5″ (49.5 cm)

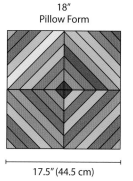

18″ Pillow Form

17.5″ (44.5 cm)

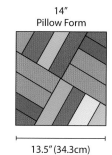

14″ Pillow Form

13.5″ (34.3cm)

Top assembly

CONSTRUCTION

All seams are sewn at ¼″ (6mm) unless otherwise noted.

Make the Pillow Front

Make your blocks to size, framed, or sashed and bordered. For a pillow top that makes a snug, plump pillow, we prefer to subtract 1″ (2.5cm) from the pillow form size and add ¼″ (6mm) seam allowance on each side—for instance, an 18″ × 18″ (45.7 × 45.7cm) pillow form would need a 17½″ × 17½″ (44.5 × 44.5cm) square pieced block. See the assembly diagram.

Sandwich and Quilt

1. Assemble the pillow top sandwich as follows:

Backing, right side down

Batting

Quilt top, right side up

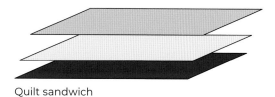

Quilt sandwich

2. Quilt the top as desired.

Make the Back Panels

1. Lay 1 rectangle of back fabric right side down and fold the top edge down ½″ (1.2cm). Press flat.

2. Fold the top over again ½″ (1.2cm), encasing the first fold. Press. *Fig. A*

3. Sew the hem closed.

4. Repeat for the second back panel.

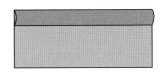

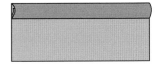

A.

Assemble Pillow

1. Lay the pillow top right side up.

2. Lay 1 back piece right side down on top of the quilt piece, making sure that the unsewn edge is even with the top of the pillow front and that the folded/sewn edge is toward the center. *Fig. B*

3. Lay the second back piece right side down on top of the quilt piece and the first back panel, making sure that the unsewn edge is even with the bottom of the pillow front and that the folded/sewn edge is toward the center the back. This panel will overlap the first one. *Fig. C*

4. Sew ¼″ (6mm) seam around the outside edge of the pillow.

5. Trim the corners to, without cutting through, the sew line.

6. Turn the finished pillow right side out through the opening.

7. Insert the pillow form.

8. Casually toss the pillow on the bed with its companion quilt or on your fainting couch to accompany the wall hanging over your fireplace mantle. (What? You don't have a fainting couch next to a huge fireplace?)

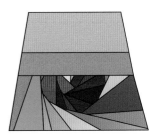

B.

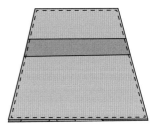

C.

TOTES CUTE TOTE

We have a thing for bags. Okay, so Shannon is the one who really has a thing for bags. Like ... *really*. Tote bags in particular are a favorite of hers for carrying with casual outfits or for toting around that extra pair of comfy shoes at events. Sure, you could also use them for grocery shopping. Either way, a household like ours can never have enough cute tote bags. Make one from the Entwined panels like we did here, but then use the schematic as a template for any blocks in any combination for your own tote that we have no doubt will be Totes Cute, too.

MATERIALS

6 Entwined panels 3½″ × 37″ (8.9 × 94cm)

Cotton/muslin: ¾ yard (69cm) for interlining

For a heavier bag, you can substitute heavy cotton bag interfacing.

Heavy cotton or canvas: ¾ yard (69cm) for lining

Heavy cotton fabric: ¼ yard for straps (23cm)

Pocket fabric: ¼ yard (23cm)

Tab fabric: ⅛ yard (11.4cm)

2-sided fusible interfacing

Drawstring or paracord: 40″ (102cm)

Drawstring toggle lock to fit the drawstring

Thread

Machine quilting in Aurifil 12-weight, color #4657

CUTTING

Cotton/muslin
Cut 1 rectangle 19″ × 37″ (48 × 94cm) for interlining.

Heavy cotton or canvas
Cut 1 rectangle 19″ × 37″ (48 × 94cm) for lining.

Heavy cotton
Cut 2 rectangles 4″ × 23″ (10 × 58.4cm) for straps.

2-sided fusible interfacing
Cut 2 strips 1″ × 23″ (2.5 × 58.4cm) for straps.

Pocket fabric
Cut 2 squares 6½″ × 6½″ (16.5 × 16.5cm) for inner pockets.

Tab fabric
Cut 2 rectangles 7″ × 4″ (18 × 10cm) for tab 1.

Cut 2 rectangles 3″ × 4″ (8 × 10cm) for tab 2.

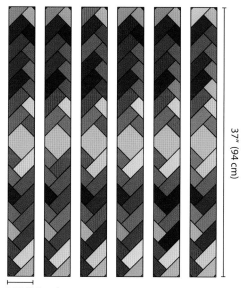

3.5″ (8.9 cm)

Tote assembly

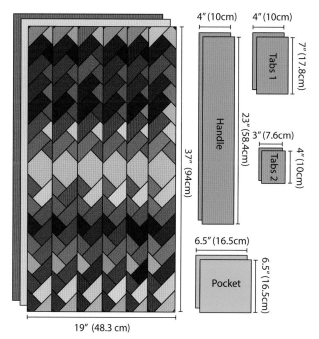

Cutting diagram

CONSTRUCTION

All seam allowances are ¼" (6mm) unless otherwise noted.

Panels

The construction for these panels is based on the Entwined block, but the longer panels come with some specific points of interest to pay attention to while you create them. See Entwined (page 51) for details.

1. Make 6 Entwined panels that are each 3½" × 37" (8.9 × 94cm). We used a 1½" (3.8cm) square for a starter piece and strips 1"–1¼" (2.5–3.2cm) wide.

2. Sew the panels together, making a 19" × 37" (48 × 94cm) rectangle. See tote assembly diagram, page 101.

Handles

1. With the wrong side facing up, fold each strip in half lengthwise and press. *Fig. A*

2. Finger-press open, again with the wrong side facing up, and fold the left and right sides to the center line. Press the sides, fold in half along the first fold, and press. *Figs. B-C*

3. Place 2-sided fusible interfacing along 1 side of the inner handle.

4. Fold it closed and press to seal.

5. Topstitch ⅛" (3mm) from the edge along both long sides. *Fig. D*

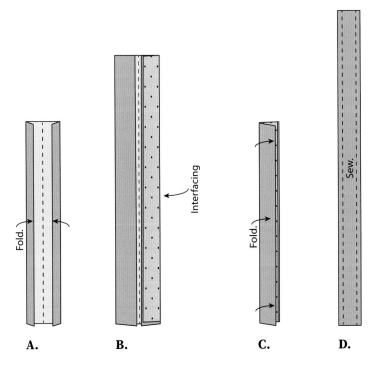

Fold.

Interfacing

Fold.

Sew.

A.   **B.**   **C.**   **D.**

Assemble the Sandwich and Quilt

1. Lay the interlining fabric on a flat surface and spray with basting spray.

2. Place the braids panel right side up on top of the interlining.

3. Fold the sandwich in half longways, right sides together.

4. Cut a 3″ × 3″ (7.6 × 7.6cm) square from the lower left and right corners of the bag on the folded edge, as shown in the diagram. *Fig. E*

5. You can hand or machine quilt your chosen pattern. We hand stitched a moyouzashi sashiko 30° grid for our quilting.

Construct the Bag Lining

Make 2 Pockets

1. Place a pocket right side down and fold ¼″ (6mm) down along the top edge. Press.

2. Repeat that fold again another ¼″ (6mm) to encase the edge, creating a rolled hem.

3. Sew down the middle of the hem to secure.

4. Repeat Steps 1–3 for the second pocket.

Lining Assembly

1. Fold the lining in half crosswise with wrong sides together. Press along the fold.

2. Cut a 3″ × 3″ (7.6 × 7.6cm) square from the lower left and right corners of the bag on the folded edge. *Fig. F*

3. Open the lining to lay flat with right side up and press flat.

4. Topstitch the pockets in place, as shown in the diagram. *Fig. G.*

Tabs

1. Place a tab 1 right side down and fold the right 4″ edge in ¼″ (6mm). Press and then sew along the edge to secure.

2. Repeat for the left side.

3. Fold it in half lengthwise and press again.

4. Repeat Steps 1–3 for the remaining tabs, hemming the 4″ edges of each.

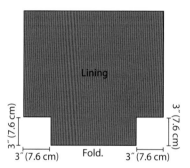

3″ (7.6 cm)   3″ (7.6 cm)   Fold.   3″ (7.6 cm)

E.

Lining

3″ (7.6 cm)   3″ (7.6 cm)   Fold.   3″ (7.6 cm)

F.

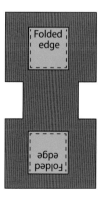

Folded edge

Folded edge

G.

Construct the Bag

1. Place the quilted bag body with right sides together and sew ½″ (1.2cm) seam on the left and right sides, from the top of the bag to the top of the cutout section. *Fig. H*

2. Press the seams open.

3. Matching the seam to the center of the cutout, sew ¼″ (6mm) seam closing the "mouth" of the left and right sides. *Fig. I*

4. Fold the top down 1″ (2.5cm) and press.

5. Turn the bag body right side out.

6. Repeat Steps 1–4 for the lining, keeping it wrong side out.

7. Insert the lining into the bag body, matching the side seams and top folded edges.

8. Insert the base of the handles between the body and the lining 1″ (2.5cm) down from the top edge and 1″–2″ (2.5–5cm) from each side. Pin in place. *Fig. J*

9. Insert the first tab 1, ½″ (1.2cm) down between the layers, centered on 1 long side between the handles. Pin in place. *Fig. K*

10. Repeat Step 9 for the second tab 1.

11. Repeat Steps 9–10 for each tab 2 on the narrow sides of the bag.

12. Topstitch 2 lines around the top edge of the bag, 1 approximately ⅛″ (3mm) from the top edge and another just shy of ½″ (1.2cm) from the top, being sure to catch all layers, handles, and tabs to secure and reinforce.

13. *Optional:* Stitch a box and X along the base of each handle where they are inserted into the top of the bag. *Fig. L*

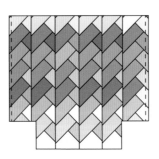

H.

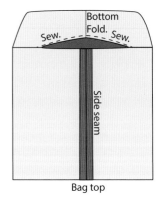

I.

J.

K.

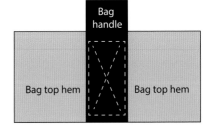

L.

Finishing

1. If desired, secure the inside bottom corners of the bag lining by making a tack stitch in each corner. This will prevent the lining from coming out of the bag when you remove your wallet to pay for your next haul at the fabric store.

2. Insert the drawstring through the tabs, securing with a drawstring toggle lock.

Drawstrings not your thing? Insert a scarf through the tabs and tie loosely to add a stylish touch and make your *Totes Cute Tote* even more totes cuter!

STAR STUFF

Those words will always be a reminder of the fact that every one of us, and every speck of matter in the universe, shares a connection that transcends space and time. Regardless of our differences on the outside, we are all part of one, infinite universe. WHEW! We can both remember reading, contemplating, and understanding those words for the first time and, honestly, having our minds blown more than a little. For our *Star Stuff* wall hanging, we linked those profound words with the visuals of the streaming trails of starlight in Van Gogh's iconic *Starry Night*.

This three-panel wall hanging uses the Oh, My Stars! blocks framed in dark blue cotton fabric hand-dyed by Jason. The fabric was dyed slightly scrunched up so the final colors would look more mottled and better resemble the sky in *Starry Night*. Muslin, instead of batting, was used in the sandwich to add stability for hanging. We then machine and hand quilted, using variegated and solid blues and yellows to add swirls of star light.

"The cosmos is also within us, we're made of star-stuff. We are a way for the cosmos to know itself." – Carl Sagan

MATERIALS

Hand-dyed or mottled blue: 4 yards (3.7m) for framing fronts and star blocks. We dyed our own fabric using dyes available at any craft store and light, neutral-colored fabric that was languishing on our shelves. It was a fun way to add another personal touch to the finished project for the result we wanted.

Hand-dyed or mottled blue: 4 yards (3.7m) for backing and tabs

Yellow scraps for stars

Muslin: 3 yards (2.8m) for interfacing

Thread
Machine sewing for quilt-top assembly:
Aurifil 50-weight, color #2784

Hand quilting: Aurifil 12-weight in shades of yellow and blue. We used colors #2740, #2775, #4655, #2140, and #3910.

CUTTING

Hand-dyed or mottled blue
Cut 24 squares 3½″ × 3½″ (8.9 × 8.9cm).

Cut 48 squares 2½″ × 2½″ (6.4 × 6.4cm).

Cut 96 squares 1½″ × 1½″ (3.8 × 3.8cm).

Yellow scraps
Cut 3 squares 3½″ × 3½″ (8.9 × 8.9cm) for center blocks.

Cut 6 squares 2½″ × 2½″ (6.4 × 6.4cm) for center blocks.

Cut 12 squares 1½″ × 1½″ (3.8 × 3.8cm) for center blocks.

Interfacing
Cut 3 rectangles 16½″ × 49½″ (41.9 × 125.7cm) for interfacing panels. (We used a lightweight muslin left over from draping garments.)

Hand-dyed or mottled blue
Cut 3 rectangles 16½″ × 49½″ (41.9 × 125.7cm) for backing panels.

Cut 9 rectangles 5″ × 6″ (12.7 × 15.2cm) for top tabs.

CONSTRUCTION

All seam allowances are ¼″ (6mm) unless otherwise noted.

Blocks

1. Construct the Oh, My Stars! blocks (page 66) for the panels (7 stars per panel):

3 stars 9½″ × 9½″ (24.1 × 24.1cm)

6 stars 6½″ × 6½″ (16.5 × 16.5cm)

12 stars 3½″ × 3½″ (8.9 × 8.9cm)

2. Lay out the stars on a large piece of fabric according to the assembly diagram. Each panel will have 1 star that is 9½″ × 9½″ (24.1 × 24.1cm), 2 stars that are 6½″ × 6½″ (16.5 × 16.5cm), and 4 stars that are 3½″ × 3½″ (8.9 × 8.9cm). Take a photo of the layout to reference as you sew the panels (see Putting It Together, page 68). We also clipped all the blocks together in order from the top to bottom of each panel. Gotta stay organized!

Panels

1. Frame each of the star sections as shown in the assembly diagram, cutting the framing pieces with seam allowances.

2. Starting with panel 1, sew the 7 individual sections together. Check the assembly diagram to ensure accuracy.

3. Repeat Steps 1–2 for the remaining 2 panels. Note that each panel has the stars placed in a different order:

Panel 2: 5″, 5″, 5″, 8″, 8″, 11″, 5″

Panel 3: 5″, 11″, 8″, 8″, 5″, 5″, 5″

Quilting

Hand or machine quilt the panels. We used free-form moyouzashi-style running stitches and Aurifil 12-weight thread to quilt our panels.

Tabs

1. Fold the tab pieces in half lengthwise with right side facing and sew a ¼″ (6mm) seam, creating a tube.

2. Press the seam open.

3. Turn the tube inside out.

4. Press the tube flat, with the seam centered on the back.

Assemble

1. Assemble the quilt sandwich of each panel as follows:

Quilt top, right side up

3 tabs, evenly spaced across the top, with the loops pointing down toward the center of the panel

Interfacing

Backing, right side down

2. Pin around the edges, including through the tabs, in preparation for sewing.

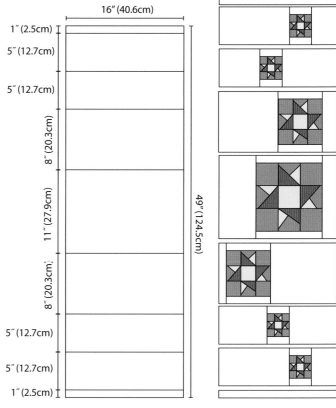

Quilt assembly for panel 1

3. Sew around the edge of the panel, leaving a 4″ (10cm) space on the bottom to turn right side out.

4. Clip the corners to just shy of the sew line and turn right side out. Use a point turner to ensure crisp corners.

5. Press and then hand sew the opening closed, using a ladder stitch or slip stitch (see Ladder Stitch, page 23).

6. Repeat for the remaining panels.

Finishing

1. Press.

2. Hang it on the gallery wall in your castle or mansion … or on your living room wall over the couch. Whatever makes you happy.

NIGHT ROOST

One of the joys of living in the Pacific Northwest is the abundance of avian wildlife. The mountains, waterways, and temperate rain forests are home to a vast array of winged creatures that we spend a considerable amount of time observing while contemplating their existence. What are they doing? Where are they going? (Yes, we have entered our sit-in-the-window-and-watch-birds era.) One of our favorite phenomena is when the crows are all heading to their night roost for the evening. Just as the sun is setting, the sky fills with their torpedo-shaped bodies propelled by gloriously inky-black corvid wings. So many fill the sky that one might believe Alfred Hitchcock was involved, but, in fact, these social birds are heading home for the evening to a skyscraper-tall tree or a cluster of evergreens on a hillside. It is a glorious sight to behold, and one we love being witness to. In the *Night Roost* wall hanging, we evoke the imagery of those birds heading to their evening respite against a field of colors inspired by our glorious sunsets.

MATERIALS

36 square 6½″ × 6½″(16.5 × 16.5cm) Fly Away Home blocks (page 55)

Black: 3 yards (2.8m) for backing, facing, and border (We used Michael Miller, Cotton Couture, color Jet Black, JETBLA-SBLK-D.)

Blue: ½ yard (46cm) (We used Cherrywood Hand Dyed Fabric—Color 0980, Jaybird.)

Dark- or muddy-green scraps: ½ yard (46cm) for first layer of blocks

Indigo: ¾ yard (69cm) for last layer of each block (We used Cherrywood Hand Dyed Fabric—Color 0905, Indigo.)

Assorted sunset color scraps: 2–3 yards (1.9–2.8m) for blocks

Batting: queen size (We used Hobbs Heirloom Premium 80/20 Black Cotton Blend Batting.)

Thread

Machine quilting in:

Aurifil 40-weight, color #2270 (top thread)

Aurifil 50-weight, color #2810 (top thread over birds)

Aurifil 50-weight, color #2692 (bobbin thread for all machine quilting)

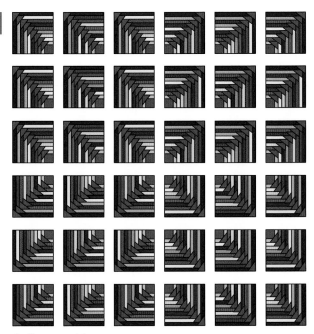

Quilt assembly

CUTTING

Starting blocks (see *Fly Away Home* block instructions)

Strips in colors as described in Materials section

Black

Cut 4 strips 2″ × 44″ (5 × 111.8cm) for borders.

Cut 1 square 42″ × 42″ (106.7 × 106.7cm) for backing.

Cut 4 strips 2½″ × 39½″ (6.4 × 100.3cm) for facing.

Cut 4 squares 4″ × 4″ (10cm) for hanging corners.

CONSTRUCTION

All seam allowances are ¼″ (6mm) unless otherwise noted.

Blocks

1. Make 36 Fly Away Home blocks, trimmed to 6½″ × 6½″ (16.5 × 16.5cm) square.

2. The initial square and bird pieces should be made from the same color of fabric to preserve the flying bird effect across the project.

3. The first 2 scrappy strips sewn to the starting square are dark or muddy green.

4. Check your dimensions often, and when you are 1 layer away from the trimmed measurements, make the final layer with dark blue strips.

Assembly

1. Lay out the blocks for Rows 1 and 2, as shown on the assembly diagram, and assemble the wall hanging as described in Putting It Together (page 68).

2. Attach the border strips according to the border instructions.

Border

This border has mitered corners ... don't worry ... it's not as scary as it sounds.

1. Mark the center of the border strips and, with right sides facing, pin the border strips to 2 sides of the project (left/right or top/bottom). *Fig. A*

2. Sew the border strips to the project, stopping ¼″ (6mm) from the corners. Backstitch to secure. *Fig. B*

3. Repeat Steps 1–2 for the remaining sides.

4. Press the border strips to the outside of the project. Leave overlapping fabric for the miters. *Fig. C*

5. For the miters, working on one corner at a time, hold the excess border fabric with right sides together and pin to secure. *Fig. D*

6. Draw a 45° angle from the corner of the project to the outside edge of the border fabric.

7. Sew along the marked 45° line. *Fig. E*

8. Before trimming, check that the mitered border lays correctly.

9. Trim excess fabric to ¼″ (6mm) seam allowance.

10. Press the seam allowance open. *Fig. F*

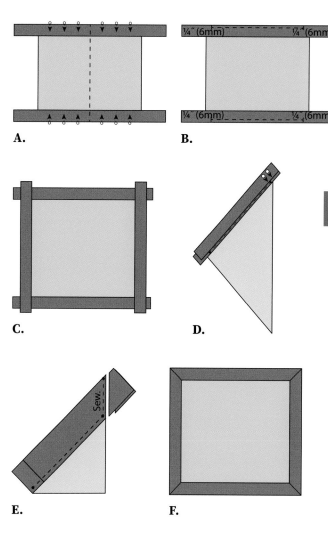

A.

B.

C.

D.

E.

F.

Final mitered border

Finishing

1. Build your quilt sandwich and pin or spray baste the layers together.

2. Quilt the layers together. We used echo quilting that followed the movement created by the "birds" in the design of the assembled blocks on our *Night Roost* wall hanging (see Quilting, page 78).

3. We used a facing for *Night Roost* to preserve the effect of the black border (see Livin' on the Edge, page 82).

4. Options: Make a rod pocket (see Just Hangin' Around, page 87), or use the Facing technique (page 83) to make hanging corners.

THE FULL MONTY

No burlesque to be seen here, but a large cast of big, beautiful, bodacious scrappy wonky quilt blocks is on full display in our *The Full Monty* quilt. Use this project as a way to showcase all of your scrappy wonky skills or pick your favorites for a custom look of your own. Then, show it off! That's what *the Full Monty* is all about!

MATERIALS

This is a scrappy quilt, so fabric amounts will vary based on your block and design choices.

Scrappy wonky blocks of your choice: 42 square 10½″ × 10½″' (26.7 × 26.7cm) blocks and 4 square 4½″ × 4½″ (11.4 × 11.4cm) blocks

Deep purple: 2½ yards (2.3m) for sashing and inner borders (We used Cherrywood Hand Dyed Fabric, color 1100 Raisin.)

Assorted fabric scraps: approximately 2 yards (1.9m), each at least 4½″ (11.4cm) wide for the border

Off-white: 3 yards (2.8m) for backing and facing (We used Robert Kaufman Fabrics, Kona Wide [108″ (274cm)], color Bone K082–1037.)

Batting: queen size (We like Hobbs Tuscany Collection 100% Wool.)

Thread

Machine quilting in Aurifil 50-weight, color #5010

CUTTING

Deep purple

Cut 2 long strips 2″ × 82½″ (5 × 209.6cm) for side inner borders.

Cut 8 long strips 2″ × 68″ (5 × 172.7cm) for horizontal sashing and top and bottom inner borders.

Cut 42 short strips 2″ × 10½″ (5 × 26.7cm) for vertical sashing.

Assorted fabric scraps

Cut 4½″-wide (11.4cm) strips of various lengths. The total border length is approximately 262″.

Off-white

Cut 1 rectangle 86″ × 97″ (218 × 246cm) for backing.

Cut 2 strips 2½″ × 89″ (6.4 × 226.1cm) for sides facing.

Cut 2 strips 2½″ × 77½″ (6.4 × 196.9cm) for top and bottom facing.

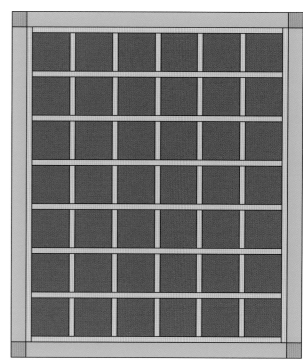

Quilt assembly

CONSTRUCTION

All seam allowances are ¼″ (6mm) unless otherwise noted.

Blocks

1. Construct 42 blocks that are each 10½″ × 10½″ (26.7 × 26.7cm). Choose the blocks you like the best or do a few of each!

2. On a design wall or the floor, arrange the blocks. Take a photo for reference and perspective.

3. Make 4 blocks of your choice that are each 4½″ × 4½″(11.4 × 11.4cm). These will be keystones in the border.

Border

To make the strip border easier to trim, we make pieces that are about the length of our longest quilting ruler or straight edge, trim them to 4″ (10cm) wide, and then sew them together into the lengths shown in the assembly diagram.

1. Choosing strips of different widths that are at least 4½″ (11.4cm) long, sew them together to create the border sections.

2. Press all seams to one side.

3. Trim the border sections to 4″ (10cm) wide.

4. Sew individual sections together, making longer strips.

5. Construct 4 strips for the border of your quilt. Make 2 that are each 82½″ (209.6cm) for the sides, and 2 that are each 71″ (180.3cm) for the top and bottom.

> ### TIP • Multipurpose Border
> This type of strip-pieced border can be used for any of the projects in this book. It is a scrap buster, and the wonky piecing makes our scrappy wonky hearts sing.

Assemble

1. Lay out the blocks for Row 1 of the quilt. See quilt assembly diagram, page 113.

2. With right sides facing, sew a short sashing piece to the right side of block 1.

3. Press the seams to the sashing.

4. With right sides facing, sew the opposite side of the same sashing piece to the left side of block 2 and press.

5. Repeat Steps 2–4, sewing sashing between sets of blocks until Row 1 is complete.

6. Repeat Steps 1–5 for all rows.

7. Lay out assembled Rows 1 and 2.

8. With right sides facing, sew a long sashing strip to the bottom of Row 1.

9. With right sides facing, sew the same long sashing strip to the top of Row 2.

10. Repeat Steps 7–9 until all rows are connected with sashing.

11. Sew an inner border to the top of Row 1 and the bottom of Row 7.

12. Sew the right and left inner borders to the long sides of the assembled quilt top.

13. Sew the right and left outer border strips to the long sides of the assembled quilt top.

14. Sew keystone blocks to the right and left ends of the top outer border strip.

15. Center the top outer border and attach it to the quilt top, making sure that the keystone seam matches the seams on the side borders.

16. Repeat Steps 14 and 15 for the bottom outer border.

17. Press the finished quilt top.

> ### TIP • Sashing Assembly
> The assembly instructions for a quilt top that includes sashing and a border can be used for any project with blocks. Create your own quilt with sashing from your favorite block or blocks or apply sashing to a pillow or wall hanging.

Finishing

1. Build your quilt sandwich and pin or spray baste the layers together.

2. Quilt the layers together. We used straight-line grid quilting on our *Full Monty*. See Quilting, page 78.

3. We used facing to keep the edges clean and neat without a visible border. See Livin' on the Edge, page 82.

PLACE

A sense of place is the effective link we all feel in relation to certain locations and environments. It's that feeling we have when we finally return home after a long trip or a hard day out there <waves arms about wildly>. Place is the culture that develops in our neighborhoods when we live in connection with those around us and actually take the time to be active participants within our community. Place tells us that we belong. Place tells us that we are home.

Place is created using Love Shack blocks in various sizes—some framed, some not. Our funky little shacks have evolved into an entire city of dwellings, complete with thriving suburbs.

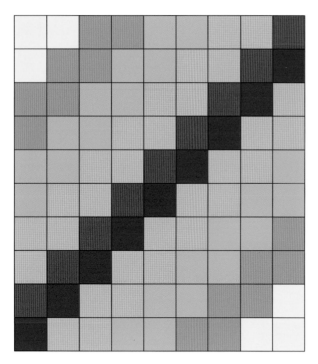

Quilt assembly

FINISHED QUILT: 90″ × 100″ (229 × 254cm)

■	Full block 18
■	Single mostly full 30
■	Single less full 22
■	Mixed single or multiple 14
□	Small single 6

MATERIALS

90 Love Shack blocks 10½″ × 10½″ (26.7 × 26.7cm) (page 45).

Soft white: about 6 yards (5.5m) for framing. (Our framing fabric was purchased years ago for a different project that never came to be. Can 6 yards [5.5m] still be considered scraps?)

Backing: 3 yards (2.8m) (We used Robert Kaufman Fabrics, Kona Wide [108″ (274cm)], color Bone K082–1037.)

Binding: 1 yard (1m), your choice; see Livin' on the Edge, page 82.

Batting: king size (We used Hobbs Tuscany Collection 100% Premium Polyester.)

Thread
Machine quilting in Aurifil 50-weight, color #2405

CUTTING

Backing
Cut 1 rectangle 98″ × 108″ (249 × 274cm).

ASSEMBLY NOTES

Place uses a variety of sizes of framed and unframed Love Shack blocks (see Squaring Up and Framing, page 31). The effect is to have a denser assembly of blocks in the center diagonal rows and then for the blocks to disperse outward toward the corners, with the space filled up with the framing fabric.

- Full blocks: The 2 center diagonal rows are made up of a total of 18 Love Shack blocks with no framing, each 10½″ × 10½″ (26.7 × 26.7cm).

- Single mostly full blocks: Moving outward toward the corners, the next 2 diagonal rows are made up of 30 Love Shack blocks that are framed on 1 or 2 sides.

- Single less-full blocks: The next 2 diagonal rows are made up of 22 medium-size Love Shack blocks that are framed on 3 or 4 sides.

- Mixed single or multiple blocks: The 2 diagonal rows just before the outside corners consist of 14 medium and small Love Shack blocks framed as combo blocks.

- Small single blocks: The outer 2 corner sections consist of 6 small framed Love Shack blocks (3 blocks in both corners), completing the dispersed effect.

CONSTRUCTION

All seam allowances are ¼″ (6mm) unless otherwise noted.

Blocks

1. Construct 90 Love Shack blocks, each trimmed to 10½″ × 10½″ (26.7 × 26.7cm) square and framed as follows (see the assembly diagram):

 18 full blocks

 30 single mostly full blocks

 22 single less-full blocks

 14 mixed single or multiple blocks

 6 small single blocks

Assemble

1. Lay out the quilt as shown in the assembly diagram (page 116) on a design wall or the floor.

2. Take a photo for reference and stack blocks in rows as they are to be assembled.

3. Lay out the blocks for Rows 1 and 2, as shown in the assembly diagram, and assemble as described in Putting It Together, page 68.

> **TIP • Check Your Photo**
> As you assemble your sections and rows, check your reference photo to ensure that you have your blocks laid out correctly.

Finishing

1. Build your quilt sandwich with batting and backing and pin or spray baste the layers together.

2. Quilt the layers together. We used a graphic straight-line quilting design for *Place*.

3. Finish the edges: We used facing to keep the edges clean and neat without a visible border. See Livin' on the Edge, page 82.

SHE KNOWS

The 1981 ode to the enigmatic eyes of the iconic Ms. Bette Davis describes not just a timeless beauty but a bold confidence that means that she knows what it takes and that what she wants will be hers. You can't help but fall in love. Yup … that sums up our obsession with the All-Seeing Eye block. We started teaching these blocks in our Quilt-As-You-Go-Go workshops, and although we thought that this was going to be a small throw, we were inexplicably compelled to return to the cutting table repeatedly to explore the scrappy wonky composition and to dive deep into the seductive color palette until this project emerged as quite a bit more than a lap throw. The pop of color unifies and draws in the observer, bringing the otherwise chaotic strips into a focus that shifts smoothly from centers to borders. The longer you look, the harder it is to turn away. To add to the irresistibility, we used a decadent plaid flannel from Robert Kaufman Fabrics as our backing.

FINISHED QUILT: 100″ × 90″ (254 × 228.6cm)

10 Blocks

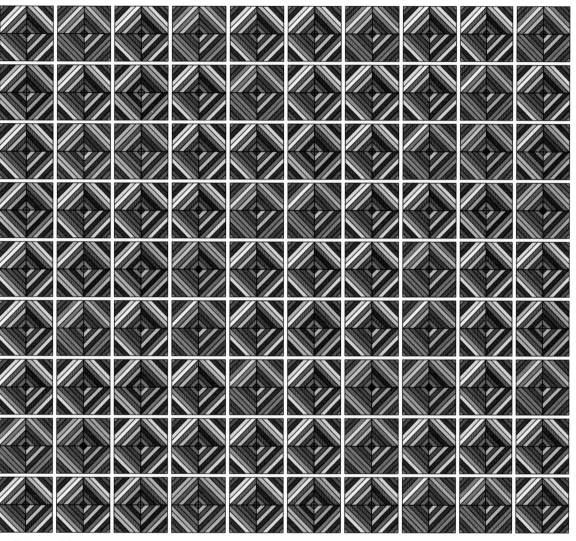

9 Blocks

Quilt assembly

SHE KNOWS

MATERIALS

Various scraps for 10½″ × 10½″ (26.7 × 26.7cm) All-Seeing Eye blocks (page 43).

Backing: 5½ yards (5.1m) (We used Robert Kaufman Fabrics, Mammoth Flannel Wide [59″ (150cm)], color Red SRKFX-20092–3.)

Binding: 1 yard (1m) (We used Michael Miller, Cotton Couture, color Jet Black JETBLA-SBLK-D.)

Batting: king size (We used Hobbs Tuscany Collection Silk.)

Thread

Machine quilting in Aurifil 50-weight, color #5010

CUTTING

Backing

Cut 2 rectangles 98″ × width of fabric (249cm × width of fabric).

Binding

Cut 11 strips 2½″ × width of fabric (6.4cm × width of fabric).

CONSTRUCTION

All seam allowances are ¼″ (6mm) unless otherwise noted.

Blocks

Make 90 All-Seeing Eye blocks (page 43), each trimmed to 10½″ × 10½″ (26.7 × 26.7cm) square.

Assemble

1. On a design wall or the floor, lay out blocks in 9 rows and 10 columns.

2. Take a photo of the layout for reference and stack the blocks in rows.

3. Lay out the blocks for Rows 1 and 2, as shown on the assembly diagram, and assemble the wall hanging as described in Putting It Together (page 68).

Finishing

1. Build your quilt sandwich and pin or spray baste the layers together.

2. Quilt the layers together. We used a 45° grid turned on point and echo quilting on *She Knows*.

3. Bind your quilt. We used 2½″ (6.4cm) binding to give this quilt a very fine ¼″ (6mm) border. See Livin' on the Edge (page 82).

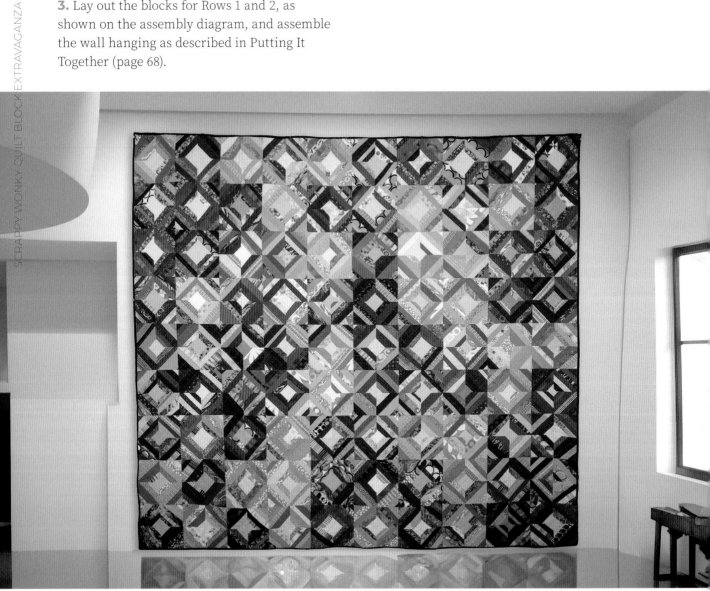

UPSON DOWNS

Rosalind Russell has always been, and will forever be, our favorite Auntie Mame. Although the entire film is one iconic moment after another (And I stepped on the ping-pong ball!), Claude's sweet daiquiris at the family's estate of Upson Downs is where we drew the name for this generously sized throw that will keep you cozy through your own ups and downs. It also makes a stunning wall hanging, just in case your own family estate (we all have those, right?) has a big open space that could use some color.

FINISHED QUILT: 74″ × 74″ (188 × 188cm)

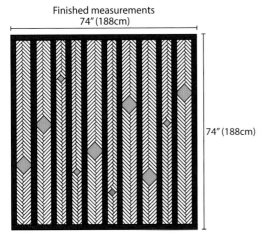

Finished measurements
74″ (188cm)

74″ (188cm)

Quilt assembly

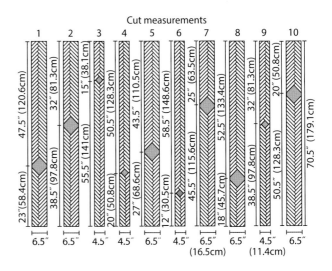

Cut measurements

MATERIALS

Assorted scraps: 1¼″–1¾″ (3.2–4.4cm) wide strips for the 6½″ (16.5cm) braid

Assorted scraps: 1″–1½″ (2.5–3.8cm) wide strips for the 4½″ (11.4cm) braid

Sashing, border, and facing: 4½ yards (4.2 m) of 42″ (107cm)-wide fabric (We used Cherrywood Hand Dyed Fabric—Color 0910, Shadow.)

Backing: 3 yards (2.8m) (We used Robert Kaufman Fabrics, Kona Wide [108″ (274cm)], color Navy K082–1243.)

Batting: queen size (We used Hobbs Heirloom Premium 80/20 Cotton/Poly Blend.)

Thread
Machine quilting in Aurifil 50-weight, color #5010

CUTTING

Assorted Scraps

Cut 6 squares 3″ × 3″ (7.6 × 7.6cm) for the 6½″ (16.5cm) braid panels.

Cut 4 squares 2″ × 2″ (5 × 5cm) for the 4½″ (11.4cm) braid panels.

Cut scrappy strips in the color palette of your choice … or in no particular color palette at all! See ish cutting guidelines for strips in Entwined, page 51.

Sashing, Border, Facing

Cut 11 strips 2½″ × 70½″ (6.4 × 179.1cm) for the sashing/borders.

Cut 6 strips 2½″ × 74½″ (6.4 × 189.2cm) for the top/bottom borders and the facing.

Backing

Cut 1 square 83″ × 83″ (211 × 211cm).

CONSTRUCTION

All seam allowances are ¼″ (6mm) unless otherwise noted.

Panels

Although the construction of these panels is based on the Entwined block, the longer panels come with some specific points of interest to pay attention to while you create them. Be sure to review those in Entwined blocks, page 51.

1. Make 6 Entwined panels (page 53), each 6½″ × 70½″ (16.5 × 179.1cm).

2. Make 4 Entwined panels, each 4½″ × 70½″ (11.4 × 179.1cm).

3. On a design wall or the floor, lay out the panels and check your design.

4. Take a photo of the final layout for reference (see Putting It Together, page 68).

5. With right sides facing, sew 1 sashing strip to the right side of panel 1.

6. Press the seams to one side.

7. With right sides facing, sew the assembled panel/sashing to the left side of strip 2.

8. Continue in this manner until all the strips are sashed.

9. With right sides facing, sew the right and left borders to the assembled quilt top.

10. Repeat Step 8 to sew the top and bottom borders to the quilt top.

11. Press the quilt top.

Finishing

1. Build your quilt sandwich and pin or spray baste the layers together.

2. Quilt the layers together. We used a combination of grid-style quilting with quilting lines spaced 1½″ (3.8cm) apart for *Upson Downs*. See Quilting, page 78.

3. We used facing for our quilt to keep the edges clean and neat without a visible border. See Livin' on the Edge, page 82.

WHAT SHE FOUND

Whether down the rabbit hole or through the looking glass, Alice always seemed to end up in the middle of a vexing situation, which always led to a grand adventure. One could say that she wasn't afraid to embrace her own creative chaos. Our scrappy purple and magnificently vibrant acid-green chessboard is created using Wonky Nine-Patch blocks sorted randomly into a madcap patchwork of which we think that even the denizens of Carroll's worlds would approve.

FINISHED QUILT: 65″ × 65″ (165 × 165cm)

13 Blocks

13 Blocks

Assembly diagram

MATERIALS

Bright green: 3 yards (2.8m) (We used Cherrywood Hand Dyed Fabric (44″ [112cm]-wide)—Color 0680, Acid Green.)

Purple scraps: approximately 4 yards (3.7m), at least 6½″ × 6½″ (16.5 × 16.5cm) square

Backing: 4¼ yards (3.9m) (We used Robert Kaufman Fabrics, Kona Cotton, color Bone K082–1037.)

Binding: ¾ yard (69cm) (We used Michael Miller, Cotton Couture, color Jet Black JETBLA-SBLK-D.)

Batting: throw size (We like Hobbs Tuscany Collection Cotton Wool.)

Thread

Machine quilting in Aurifil 50-weight, color #5010

CUTTING

Bright Green
Cut 85 squares, each 6½″ × 6½″ (16.5 × 16.5cm).

Purple scraps
Cut 85 squares, each 6½″ × 6½″ (16.5 × 16.5cm).

Binding
Cut 8 strips, each 2½″(6.4cm) x width of fabric, to make 270″ (686cm) of binding.

CONSTRUCTION

All seam allowances are ¼″ (6mm) unless otherwise noted.

Blocks

1. Using the acid-green and purple squares, construct 169 Wonky Nine-Patch blocks (page 64). There will be 1 extra block.

2. Trim the blocks to each be 5½″ × 5½″ (14 × 14cm) square.

Assemble

1. On a design wall or the floor, lay out the blocks in 13 rows and 13 columns. Make sure to alternate blocks so colored sections do not touch (that is, if the first block of the first row has 5 acid-green sections, it is followed by a block with 4 acid green sections, and so forth).

2. Take a photo of the final layout for reference and stack the blocks in rows.

3. Continue to assemble the quilt top as described in Putting It Together, page 68.

Finishing

1. Build your quilt sandwich and pin or spray baste the layers together.

2. Quilt the layers together. We used straight-line quilting on our *What She Found*. See Quilting, page 78.

3. Bind your quilt. We used 2½″ (6.4cm) binding from the back to the front, giving this quilt a visible ¼″ (6mm) border reminiscent of a chessboard. See Livin' on the Edge, page 82.

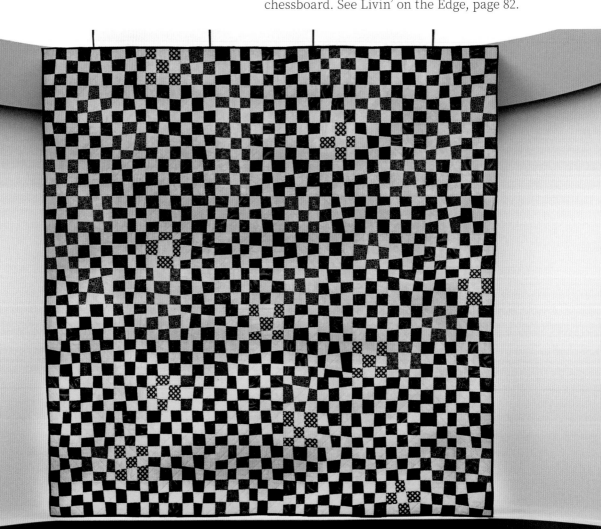

THE ROSE TATTOO

The fiery passion and deep contralto of Anna Magnani—the magnificent Magnani—inspired men to emblazon the namesake rose of her character, Serafina Delle Rose, ontheir chests. In reality, nobody really wants the life of a Tennessee Williams character, but a hint of fervor and drama is always a good thing. To that end, we present *The Rose Tattoo* jacket, featuring subtle colors embellished with Scrappy Wonky Roses to remind you that everyone, regardless of gender, has a little bit of the romantic, sultry ingénue within.

SIZES

XS (S, M, L, XL, 2X, 3X, 4X, 5X, 6X)

To fit measured bust: 28″ (32, 36, 40, 44, 48, 52, 56, 60, 64) / 71.1cm (81.3, 91.4, 101.6, 111.8, 121.9, 132.1, 142.2, 152.4, 162.6)

MATERIALS

Jacket: 111 (118, 118, 139,145, 160, 160, 160, 160, 160) 5½″ × 5½″ (14 × 14cm) Good Neighbors blocks

Rose blocks:

1 single block 6½″ × 6½″ (16.5 × 16.5cm)

1 combo block 6½″ × 6½″ (16.5 × 16.5cm)

4 single blocks 5½″ × 5½″ (14 × 14cm)

Lining: 1½ yards (1½, 1¾, 1¾, 2, 2, 2, 2¼, 2¼, 2½) / 1.4m (1.4, 1.7, 1.7, 1.9, 1.9, 1.9, 2.1, 2.1, 2.3) (We used Cherrywood Hand Dyed Fabric—Color W02, Lily.)

Collar/Cuff: 2 yards /1.9 m for all sizes. (We used Cherrywood Hand Dyed Fabric—Color W02, Lily.)

Batting: queen size (We used Hobbs Thermore.)

1″ (25mm) bias tape: 4 yards (3.7m) fusible bias tape, or cut bias binding for the seams

1½″ (38mm) bias tape: 2 yards (1.9m) fusible bias tape, or cut bias binding for the hem

5 yards (4.6m) fusible medium-weight interfacing

Thread
Machine quilting in Aurifil 50-weight, color #2423

CUTTING

Use the cutting diagram and chart provided for initial cuts.

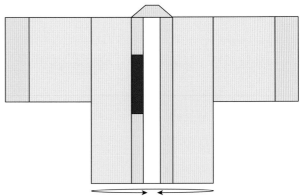

Finished Measurements: 33 (37, 41, 45, 49, 53, 57, 61, 65, 69)″ / 83.8 (94, 104.1, 114.3, 124.5, 134.6, 144.8, 154.9, 165.1, 175.3) cm

Finished sizes

NOTE • Pattern Notes

• Sizes on the schematic are shown as XS (S, M, L, XL, 2X, 3X, 4X, 5X, 6X). It may be beneficial to highlight your selected size throughout the pattern prior to measuring and cutting. All schematic measurements are given in inches and centimeters for your convenience.

• All sewn and pressed garment assembly seams are ½″ (1.2cm).

• Quilting should be done on individual components before sewing/overlocking garment pieces together.

• This jacket does not have an additional lining beyond the backing of the sandwich. To keep internal seams from fraying, we recommend using a Hong Kong finish to seal the seams (see Hong Kong Finish, page 24), using the 1″ (25mm) bias tape. An overlock stitch along the edges is also an option.

• *right side* and *wrong side* in this pattern refer to which side faces the public.

Cutting Diagram

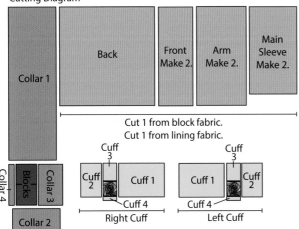

Rose Tattoo Cutting Chart

	XS	S	M	L	XL
Back body panel	17½″ × 28″	19½″ × 29″	21½″ × 30″	23½″ × 30″	25½″ × 30½″
	44.5 × 71.1cm	49.5 × 73.7cm	54.6 × 76.2cm	59.7 × 76.2cm	64.8 × 77.5cm
Front body panel	6¼″ × 28″	7″ × 28″	7¾″ × 30″	8½″ × 30″	9½″ × 30½″
	15.9 × 71.1cm	17.8 × 71.1cm	19.7 × 76.2cm	21.6 × 76.2cm	24.1 × 77.5cm
COLLAR					
collar 1	15″ × 39¼″	15″ × 41¾″	15″ × 44¼″	15″ × 44¾″	15″ × 45¾″
	38.1 × 99.7cm	38.1 × 106cm	38.1 × 112.4cm	38.1 × 113.7cm	38.1 × 116.2cm
collar 2	15″ × 10″	15″ × 10″	15″ × 10″	15″ × 10″	15″ × 10″
	38.1 × 25.4cm	38.1 × 25.4cm	38.1 × 25.4cm	38.1 × 25.4cm	38.1 × 25.4cm
collar 3	7¾″ × 12½″	7¾″ × 12½″	7¾″ × 12½″	7¾″ × 12½″	7¾″ × 12½″
	19.7 × 31.8cm	19.7 × 31.8cm	19.7 × 31.8cm	19.7 × 31.8cm	19.7 × 31.8cm
collar 4	1¾″ × 12½″	1¾″ × 12½″	1¾″ × 12½″	1¾″ × 12½″	1¾″ × 12½″
	4.4 × 31.8cm	4.4 × 31.8cm	4.4 × 31.8cm	4.4 × 31.8cm	4.4 × 31.8cm
collar interfacing	14½″ × 59¼″	14½″ × 61¼″	14½″ × 64¼″	14½″ × 64¾″	14½″ × 65¾″
	36.8 × 150.5cm	36.8 × 155.6cm	36.8 × 163.2cm	36.8 × 164.5cm	36.8 × 167cm
Sleeve	7″ × 27″	8″ × 28″	8¾″ × 28″	9″ × 28″	9¼″ × 28″
	17.8 × 68.6cm	20.3 × 71.1cm	22.2 × 71.1cm	22.9 × 71.1cm	23.5 × 71.1cm
CUFF					
cuff 1	16¾″ × 13″	17¼″ × 13″	17¼″ × 13″	17¼″ × 13″	17¼″ × 13″
	42.5 × 33cm	43.8 × 33cm	43.8 × 33cm	43.8 × 33cm	43.8 × 33cm
cuff 2	6¾″ × 13″	7¼″ × 13″	7¼″ × 13″	7¼″ × 13″	7¼″ × 13″
	17.1 × 33cm	18.4 × 33cm	18.4 × 33cm	18.4 × 33cm	18.4 × 33cm
cuff 3	5½″ × 6¾″	5½″ × 6¾″	5½″ × 6¾″	5½″ × 6¾″	5½″ × 6¾″
	14 × 17.1cm	14 × 17.1cm	14 × 17.1cm	14 × 17.1cm	14 × 17.1cm
cuff 4	5½″ × 1¾″	5½″ × 1¾″	5½″ × 1¾″	5½″ × 1¾″	5½″ × 1¾″
	14 × 4.4cm	14 × 4.4cm	14 × 4.4cm	14 × 4.4cm	14 × 4.4cm
cuff interfacing	6½″ × 27½″	6½″ × 28½″	6½″ × 28½″	6½″ × 28½″	6½″ × 28½″
	16.5 × 69.9cm	16.5 × 72.4cm	16.5 × 72.4cm	16.5 × 72.4cm	16.5 × 72.4cm
cuff length finished	6″ (15.2cm)	6″ (15.2cm)	6″ (15.2cm)	6″ (15.2cm)	6″ (15.2cm)
cuff width finished	27″ (68.6)	28″ (71.1cm)	28″ (71.1cm)	28″ (71.1cm)	28″ (71.1cm)

Rose Tattoo Cutting Chart (continued)

	2X	3X	4X	5X	6X
Back body panel	27½″ × 31″	29½″ × 31½″	31½″ × 32″	33½″ × 32″	35½″ × 32″
	69.9 × 78.7cm	74.9 × 80cm	80 × 81.3cm	85.1 × 81.3cm	90.2 × 81.3cm
Front body panel	10⅛″ × 31″	11″ × 31½″	12″ × 28″	12¾″ × 32″	13¼″ × 32″
	25.7 × 78.7cm	27.9 × 80cm	30.5 × 81.3cm	32.4 × 81.3cm	33.7 × 81.3cm
COLLAR					
collar 1	15″ × 47½″	15″ × 48¾″	15″ × 49¾″	15″ × 50¼″	15″ × 51¼″
	38.1 × 120.7cm	38.1 × 123.8cm	38.1 × 126.4cm	38.1 × 127.6cm	38.1 × 130.2cm
collar 2	15″ × 10″	15″ × 10″	15″ × 10″	15″ × 10″	15″ × 10″
	38.1 × 25.4cm	38.1 × 25.4cm	38.1 × 25.4cm	38.1 × 25.4cm	38.1 × 25.4cm
collar 3	7¾″ × 12½″	7¾″ × 12½″	7¾″ × 12½″	7¾″ × 12½″	7¾″ × 12½″
	19.7 × 31.8cm	19.7 × 31.8cm	19.7 × 31.8cm	19.7 × 31.8cm	19.7 × 31.8cm
collar 4	1¾″ × 12½″	1¾″ × 12½″	1¾″ × 12½″	1¾″ × 12½″	1¾″ × 12½″
	4.4 × 31.8cm	4.4 × 31.8cm	4.4 × 31.8cm	4.4 × 31.8cm	4.4 × 31.8cm
collar interfacing	14½″ × 67½″	14½″ × 68¾″	14½″ × 69¾″	14½″ × 70¼″	14½″ × 71¼″
	36.8 × 171.5cm	36.8 × 174.6cm	36.8 × 177.2cm	36.8 × 178.4cm	36.8 × 181cm
Sleeve	9½″ × 30″	9½″ × 30″	10″ × 30″	10″ × 30″	10″ × 30″
	24.1 × 76.2cm	24.8 × 76.2cm	25.4 × 76.2cm	25.4 × 76.2cm	25.4 × 76.2cm
CUFF					
cuff 1	18¼″ × 13″	18¼″ × 13″	18¼″ × 13″	18¼″ × 13″	18¼″ × 13″
	46.4 × 33cm	46.4 × 33cm	46.4 × 33cm	46.4 × 33cm	46.4 × 33cm
cuff 2	8¼″ × 13″	8¼″ × 13″	8¼″ × 13″	8¼″ × 13″	8¼″ × 13″
	21 × 33cm	21 × 33cm	21 × 33cm	21 × 33cm	21 × 33cm
cuff 3	5½″ × 6¾″	5½″ × 6¾″	5½″ × 6¾″	5½″ × 6¾″	5½″ × 6¾″
	14 × 17.1cm	14 × 17.1cm	14 × 17.1cm	14 × 17.1cm	14 × 17.1cm
cuff 4	5½″ × 1¾″	5½″ × 1¾″	5½″ × 1¾″	5½″ × 1¾″	5½″ × 1¾″
	14 × 4.4cm	14 × 4.4cm	14 × 4.4cm	14 × 4.4cm	14 × 4.4cm
cuff interfacing	6½″ × 30½″	6½″ × 30½″	6½″ × 30½″	6½″ × 30½″	6½″ × 30½″
	16.5 × 77.5cm	16.5 × 77.5cm	16.5 × 77.5cm	16.5 × 77.5cm	16.5 × 77.5cm
cuff length finished	6″ (15.2cm)	6″ (15.2cm)	6″ (15.2cm)	6″ (15.2cm)	6″ (15.2cm)
cuff width finished	30″ (76.2cm)	30″ (76.2cm)	30″ (76.2cm)	30″ (76.2cm)	30″ (76.2cm)

CONSTRUCTION

All seam allowances are ½″ (1.2cm) unless otherwise noted.

Blocks

1. Make 111 (118, 118, 139,145, 160, 160, 160, 160, 160) Good Neighbors blocks, each 5½″ × 5½″ (14 × 14cm) (page 40).

2. Make 1 single Scrappy Wonky Rose block that is 6½″ × 6½″ (16.5 × 16.5cm).

3. Make 1 combo Wonky Rose block that is 6½″ × 6½″(16.5 × 16.5cm).

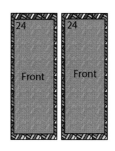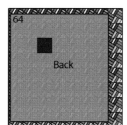

Block assembly

4. Make 4 single Scrappy Wonky Rose blocks, each 5½″ × 5½″ (14 × 14cm) (page 59).

5. Lay out the Good Neighbors blocks as shown in the block assembly diagram, swapping out Good Neighbors blocks for Scrappy Wonky Rose blocks on the back panel, as shown in the assembly diagram, or as your design sense dictates.

6. Assemble the blocks into panels, as shown in the block assembly diagram.

Cut Main Panels

1. Using the cutting chart (page 129), cut back and front pieces from assembled block panels; cut the lining from lining fabric; cut cuffs and collar pieces.

2. Spray the wrong side of the back panel with basting spray and lay on batting, being careful to smooth and adjust it as needed.

3. Trim the batting to back panel size.

4. Complete the quilt sandwich: Using basting spray, place the lining on the batting, right side up. Be sure that the edges match up perfectly.

5. Repeat for the remaining main panels.

Back Neck Drop and Shoulder Slope

S	M	L	XL	2X	3X	4X	5X
6.5	7	7.5	7.5	8.25	8.5	8.5	9

1. Fold the back panel in half and mark the center point.

2. Open the back panel right side up and make a mark 1″ (2.5cm) down from the center point you just marked.

3. Draw the back neckline measurement from the table, centered on the center point mark. Mark the left and right ends of this line on the cut edge of the fabric.

4. On the left side of the back, use a curved ruler to draw a gentle curve connecting the outside point of the back neckline mark to the corresponding center back neck drop line. Only draw this curve on one side.

5. Fold the back panel in half again and cut along the back neck drop line, cutting through all the layers of folded fabric.

> **TIP • Household Goods**
> If you are worried about drawing this curve free-hand and don't have a tailor's curve handy, you can use a plate from the kitchen as a template to help with the shape.

Quilt the Main Panels

1. Using straight-line quilting 2″ (5cm) apart at a 30° angle, quilt the main body piece layers together.

2. Square up pieces, if needed.

Attach the Fronts to the Back

1. With right sides facing, starting from the outside shoulder and sewing toward the inside edge and back neckline, sew the shoulder seams, attaching front panels to the back panel.

2. Press the shoulder seams open.

3. Encase the raw shoulder seams using a Hong Kong Finish (page 24).

Assemble the Cuff Panel

1. Following the cuff schematic, assemble 2 cuffs from the collar/cuff pieces and 2 Scrappy Rose blocks, each trimmed to 5½″ × 5½″ (14 × 14cm).

2. Attach the interfacing to the wrong side of each cuff, following the manufacturer's instructions.

Attach the Cuffs to the Sleeves

1. Fold the cuff in half lengthwise right side out and press. Open the cuff.

2. With the wrong side facing up, fold and press ½″ (1.2cm) seam allowance along the long edge, away from the rose insert.

3. Holding the raw (unfolded) edge of the cuff to the raw edge of the sleeve, with the right sides facing each other, pin or clip the cuff to the sleeve.

Cuff Layout

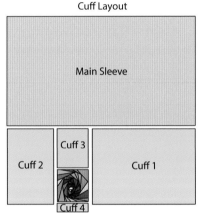

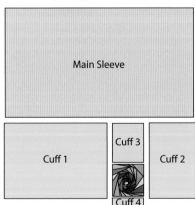

Cuff schematic

4. Sew the first side of the cuff into place using ½″ (1.2mm) seam allowance.

5. Press the seam toward the cuff.

6. Fold the cuff in half lengthwise along the pressed line so the right side of the cuff is facing out and the ½″ (1.2cm) folded/pressed seam allowance covers the raw edge. This will encase the raw seam.

7. Pin the cuff into place, being careful to pin flat so as not to skew the 2 sides of the cuff while sewing.

8. Stitch-in-the-ditch through the seam on the right side or topstitch a scant ¼″ (6mm) along the folded edge, sewing through the ½″ (1.2cm) folded seam on the backside.

9. Repeat Steps 1–8 for the second cuff.

Attach the Assembled Sleeves

1. Lay open the garment body with the right side facing up.

2. Fold the sleeve in half lengthwise and mark the center of the sleeve at the top.

3. Match the center mark on the sleeve to the shoulder seam and pin into place, right sides facing.

4. Sew the sleeve in place.

5. Repeat Steps 2–4 with the second sleeve.

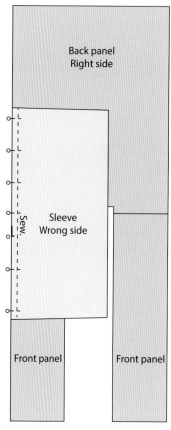

Attach the sleeves to the body.

Sew the Underside of the Sleeve and Sides

1. Turn the jacket inside out so the right side of the sleeve and the body of the jacket are facing each other.

2. Pin the side seams of the jacket body together.

3. Pin the underside seam of the sleeves together.

4. Starting from the bottom of the garment, sew the side seam up to the sleeve opening.

5. Continue to sew along the bottom seam of the sleeve to the cuff.

6. Repeat for the second sleeve.

7. Cover the underarm and side seams by using a Hong Kong Finish (page 24).

8. Turn the garment inside out and cover the armhole seams, again using a Hong Kong Finish or overcast/zigzag.

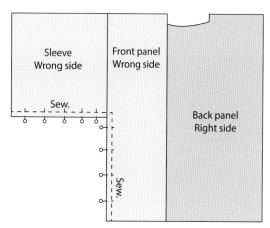

Sew the sides and underside of the sleeves.

Assemble the Collar Panels

1. With right sides facing, sew the top of the collar 2 left panel to the bottom of the collar front insert. Press the seams to one side.

2. In the same manner, with right sides facing, attach the remaining front collar 1 piece to the assembled panel. Press the seams to one side.

3. With right sides facing, sew the collar back to the front along the left side only. Press the seam open.

4. Attach the interfacing to the wrong side of the assembled collar, following the manufacturer's instructions.

5. With wrong side up, fold the short ends in ½" (1.2cm) and press.

6. Fold the collar in half lengthwise and press flat.

Attach Collar

1. Fold the collar in half lengthwise and press.

2. With wrong side facing up, press ½" (1.2cm) seam allowance along the long edge with the kogin panels.

3. Fold the collar in half crosswise and mark the center with a pin or marking pen. This is the center back neck of the collar.

4. Mark the center back of the neckline on the back piece.

5. Holding the raw (unfolded) edge of the collar to the raw edge of the neckline, with right sides facing each other, pin the center mark on the collar to the center mark on the neckline. *Fig. A*

6. Working from the center out, pin the rest of the collar into place.

7. Sew the first side of the collar into place.

> **TIP • Easy Does It!**
> When sewing the collar into place, sew just like you pinned—from the center out—to ensure that the collar lays evenly along the neckline.

8. Press the seam toward the outside of the collar. *Fig. B*

9. Fold the collar in half lengthwise along the first pressed line so the right side is facing out and ½" (1.2cm) seam covers the seam just sewn. This will encase the front edge of the raw seam.

10. Pin the collar into place, being careful to pin the collar flat so as not to skew the 2 sides of the collar while sewing.

11. From the right side of the garment, topstitch ⅛" (3mm) from the folded edge, being sure to sew through the ½" (1.2cm) folded seam and the raw seam.

> **NOTE • Use an Edge-Stitch Foot**
> We like using an edge-stitch foot for this process to keep the seam super-straight.

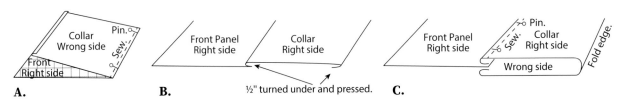

A. Collar Wrong side / Pin. / Sew. / Front Right side

B. Front Panel Right side / Collar Right side / ½" turned under and pressed.

C. Front Panel Right side / Pin. / Sew. / Collar Right side / Wrong side / Fold edge.

Bind the Bottom Hem

1. With right sides facing each other, place the opened/flat 1½″ (38mm) bias tape along the entire bottom hem ¼″ (6mm) seam. Be careful to not stretch the tape.

2. Sew ¼″ (6mm) seam along the entire bottom hem.

3. Fold the bias tape over the seam, finger-pressing if needed.

4. Turning to the inside of the garment, with the wrong sides facing, fold the remaining raw edge of the tape to the center line and fold the tape over the fabric, encasing the raw edge.

5. Pin the tape into place.

6. From the front of the garment, stitch-in-the-ditch along the sewn tape, being sure to catch the folded edge on the inside. You can also slipstitch or whipstitch the back edge closed.

7. OR use your favorite quilt binding method.

Final Touches

Press or steam the garment. Now, it's time to don your Rose Tattoo and show off your magnificent work! And get accustomed to saying, "Thank you, I made it!"

FEYWILD

Both of us spent family road trips hearing, "If you got your nose out of that book, you might see something." Yes, we were both (and still very much are) book people. Books were the perfect escape, and, more often than not, they contained tales of epic quests by Tolkien, dragons soaring through the skies of McCaffrey, battles for hidden lands created by Le Guin, and the classic triumphs of good over evil by Cooper and Lewis. Deep into the worlds of those books, we escaped. It wasn't difficult to imagine sitting by the banks of a quiet river and drifting off into dreams to awaken in the lush realm of the Feywild. Our Feywild vest is a nod to those dreamers who still live within our very souls, who draw us again and again out into the wilds of the mountains and forests that surround us in our Seattle home.

SIZES

XS (S, M, L, XL, 2X, 3X, 4X, 5X, 6X)

To fit measured bust: 28″ (32, 36, 40, 44, 48, 52, 56, 60, 64) / 71.1cm (81.3, 91.4, 101.6, 111.8, 121.9, 132.1, 142.2, 152.4, 162.6)

MATERIALS

Vest fabric: 50 (50, 50, 65, 65, 65, 65, 65, 65, 65) Down on the Corner blocks 5½″ × 5½″ (14 × 14cm)

Various scraps for block strips

Corner blocks: ¼ yard (23cm) (We used Cherrywood Hand Dyed Fabric—Color 0680, Acid Green.)

Side panel and sashing fabric: 2¾ yards (2.6m) (We used Cherrywood Hand Dyed Fabric— Color 1100, Raisin.)

Lining: 1½ yards (1½, 1½, 2, 2, 2, 2, 2, 2) / 1.4m (1.4, 1.4, 1.9, 1.9, 1.9, 1.9, 1.9, 1.9, 1.9) (We again used Cherrywood Hand Dyed Fabric – Color 1100, Raisin.)

Collar: 1 yard (1, 1, 1, 1, 1, 1, 1, 1¼, 1¼) / 1m (1, 1, 1, 1, 1, 1, 1, 1.2, 1.2) (Of course, we used Cherrywood Hand Dyed Fabric—Color 1100, Raisin.)

Batting: queen size (We used Hobbs Thermore.)

1″ (25mm) bias tape: 4 yards (3.7m) fusible bias tape, or cut bias binding for seams

1½″ (38mm) bias tape: 2 yards (1.9m) fusible bias tape, or cut bias binding for hem

Fusible medium-weight interfacing:

Thread

Machine quilting in Aurifil 50-weight, color #5010

CUTTING

1. Use the cutting table provided on the next page for initial cuts.

2. Cut strips of 1″ (2.5cm) sashing long enough for assembly.

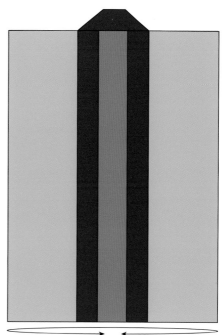

Finished Measurements: 28 (32, 36, 40, 44, 48, 52, 56, 60, 64)″
71.1 (81.3, 91.4, 101.6, 111.8, 121.9, 132.1, 142.2, 152.4, 162.6) cm

Finished sizes

NOTE • Pattern Notes

• Sizes on the schematic are shown as XS (S, M, L, XL, 2X, 3X, 4X, 5X, 6X). It may be beneficial to highlight your selected size throughout the pattern prior to measuring and cutting. All schematic measurements are given in inches and centimeters for your convenience.

• All sewn and pressed seams are ½″ (1.2cm) unless otherwise noted.

• Quilting should be done on individual components before sewing/overlocking garment pieces together.

• This jacket does not have an additional lining beyond the backing of the sandwich. To keep internal seams from fraying, we recommend using a Hong Kong finish to seal the seams (see Hong Kong Finish, page 24). An overlock stitch along the edges is also an option.

• Once the seams are pressed open or to the side, you can topstitch or use a prick stitch to secure them further.

• *right side* and *wrong side* in this pattern refer to which side faces the public.

Feywild Vest Sizing Worksheet

	XS	S	M	L	XL
COLLAR	9″ × 61″	10″ × 63½″	10″ × 66″	11″x 66½″	11″ × 67½″
	22.9 × 154.9cm	25.4 × 161.3cm	25.4 × 167.6cm	27.9 × 168.9cm	27.9 × 171.5cm
BACK	16″ × 28″	16½″ × 29″	18″ × 30″	18½″ × 30″	19½″ × 30½″
	40.6 × 71.1cm	41.9 × 73.7cm	45.7 × 76.2cm	47 × 76.2cm	49.5 × 77.5cm
FRONTS	5½″ × 28″	5½″ × 29″	6″ × 30″	6″ × 30″	6½″ × 30½″
	14 × 71.1cm	14 × 73.7cm	15.2 × 76.2cm	15.2 × 76.2cm	16.5 × 77.5cm
SIDE PANELS	2½″ × 18″	2½″ × 18″	3¾″ × 19″	5¾″ × 18½″	5¾″ × 18½″
	6.4 × 45.7cm	6.4 × 45.7cm	9.5 × 48.3cm	14.6 × 47cm	14.6 × 47cm

	2X	3X	4X	5X	6X
COLLAR	11″ × 69¼″	13″ × 70½″	13″ × 71½″	14″ × 72″	14″ × 73″
	27.9 × 175.9cm	33 × 179.1cm	33 × 181.6cm	35.6 × 182.9cm	35.6 × 185.4cm
BACK	19½″ × 31″	20″ × 31½″	20″ × 32″	20½″ × 32″	21″ × 32″
	49.5 × 78.7cm	50.8 × 80cm	50.8 × 81.3cm	52.1 × 81.3cm	53.3 × 81.3cm
FRONTS	6½″ × 31″	6¾″ × 31½″	6¾″ × 32″	7″ × 32″	7″ × 32″
	16.5 × 78.7cm	17.1 × 80cm	17.1 × 81.3cm	17.8 × 81.3cm	17.8 × 81.3cm
SIDE PANELS	6¾″ × 18½″	7¾″ × 18½″	8¾″ × 19″	8¾″ × 18″	9″ × 18″
	17.1 × 47cm	19.7 × 47cm	22.2 × 48.3cm	22.2 × 45.7cm	22.8 × 45.7cm

Trimming Chart

CONSTRUCTION

All seam allowances are ½″ (1.2cm) unless otherwise noted.

Blocks

1. Make 50 (50, 50, 65, 65, 65, 65, 65, 65, 65) Down on the Corner blocks, each 5½″ × 5½″ (14 × 14cm) (page 49). These should be made with similar colorways, and all should have the same color/ fabric for each corner piece.

2. Lay out and assemble Down on the Corner blocks on point, as shown in the block assembly diagram.

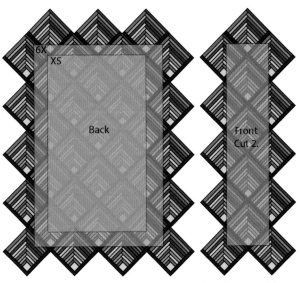

Block assembly

Cut the Main Panels

1. Using the cutting table, cut back and front panels from assembled Down on the Corner panels and cut the lining for all pieces from lining fabric.

2. Spray the wrong side of the back panel with basting spray and lay on batting, being careful to smooth and adjust it as needed.

3. Trim batting to the back panel size.

4. Complete the quilt sandwich using basting spray, placing the lining on the batting right side up. Be sure that your fabric is smooth and that piece edges match up perfectly.

5. Repeat for the remaining main panels.

Back Neck Table

S	M	L	XL	2X	3X	4X	5X
6.5″	7″	7.5″	7.5″	8.25″	8.5″	8.5″	9″

Back Neckline Table

Back Neck Drop

1. Fold the back panel in half and mark the center point.

2. Open the back panel right side up and make a mark 1″ (2.5cm) down from the center point just marked.

3. Draw the back neckline measurement from the table, centered on the center point mark. Mark the left and right ends of this line on the cut edge of the fabric.

4. On the left side of the back, use a curved ruler to draw a gentle curve connecting the outside point of the back neckline mark to the corresponding center back neck drop line. Only draw this curve on 1 side.

5. Fold the back panel in half again and cut along the back neck drop line, cutting through all the layers of folded fabric.

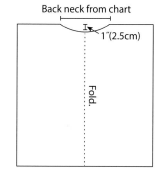

Back neck from chart

1″(2.5cm)

Fold.

> ### TIP • Household Goods
> If you are worried about drawing this curve free-hand, you can use a plate from the kitchen as a template to help with the shape.

Shoulder Slope

BACK PANEL SHOULDER SLOPE

1. On the left and right edges of the back panel, measure down 2″ (5cm) and mark (Mark A).

2. Measure and make a mark 2″ (5cm) from the outside edge of the back neckline from previous steps (Mark B); see the shoulder slope diagram.

3. Draw a straight line connecting Mark A to Mark B.

4. Cut along this line, creating the shoulder slope.

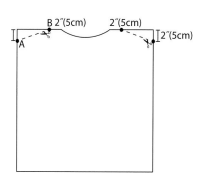

B 2″(5cm)   2″(5cm)   2″(5cm)

A

Shoulder Slope Diagram

FRONT PANEL SHOULDER SLOPE

1. Lay the front panels right side up next to one another, as they will be worn.

2. On the left edge of the left front panel, measure down 2″ (5cm) and make a mark (Mark A).

3. Measure 2″ (5cm) from the inside edge of the front panel and make a mark (Mark B).

4. Repeat Mark A and Mark B on the right front panel.

5. Draw a straight line connecting Mark A to Mark B on each front panel.

6. Cut along this line, making a slope that matches the back panel.

Quilt the Main Panels

1. Using the straight-line or free-motion style, quilt each main body piece.

2. Trim pieces, if needed, to the post-quilting size in the Trimming Chart.

Create a Slit Vent with Facing

1. With right side facing up, mark a slit opening 3″ (7.6cm) from the bottom center of the side panel. *Fig. A*

2. Cut vent facing 3½″ × 2″ (9 × 5cm) from lining fabric or a fun fabric scrap.

3. With the vent facing right side down, turn under the edges ¼″ (6mm) and press to secure. *Fig. B*

4. Fold the facing in half crosswise and finger-press to gently crease.

5. With the vent facing wrong side up, make a 3″ (7.6cm) mark starting from the bottom edge along the center line for the slit opening. *Fig. C*

6. With the facing and side panel fabric right sides together, carefully line up the marks for the slit.

7. Machine stitch a scant ⅛″ (3mm) around the cutting line from the bottom of the fabric pivoting at the top and returning back to the bottom at the other side of the line. *Fig. D*

> **TIP • Edge-Stitch Foot to the Rescue**
> We use an edge-stitch foot (10C or 10D for BERNINA machines). Move the needle position to –2 so you will sew close to the left edge of the marked line. This is where the magic comes in: Once you have your needle position set to –2, follow your marked line with the foot's guide.
>
> If you do not have an edge foot, do your best to stitch as straight as possible ⅛″ (3mm) next to the line.

8. Cut through the slit mark without cutting through the stitches.

9. Turn the facing to the inside. Smooth by hand and then press flat. *Fig. E*

10. Topstitch ⅛″ (3mm) along the slit opening to secure.

A.

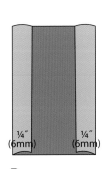

¼″ (6mm)   ¼″ (6mm)

B.

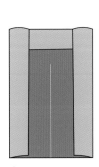

C.

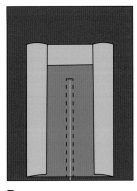

D.

E.

Attach the Fronts to the Back at the Shoulders

1. With right sides facing, starting from the outside shoulder and sewing toward the inside edge and back neckline, sew the shoulder seams, attaching the front panels to the back panel.

2. Press the shoulder seams open.

3. Encase the raw shoulder seams using a Hong Kong Finish (page 24).

Attach Side Panels

1. With right sides facing, place 1 side panel on the left front side panel, matching the bottoms. Pin in place.

2. Sew the seam and press open.

3. Repeat for the right side of the vest.

4. With right sides facing, place the side panel on the corresponding edge of the back panel, matching the bottom. Pin in place.

5. Sew the seam and press open.

6. Repeat for the right side of the vest.

7. Cover all side seams with the 1″ (25mm) bias binding and a Hong Kong Finish (page 24).

Attach the Collar

1. Fold the collar in half lengthwise and press.

2. With wrong side facing up, press ½″ (1.2cm) seam allowance along 3 sides of the collar, leaving 1 long edge raw.

3. Fold the collar in half lengthwise and mark the center line with a pin or fabric marking tool. This is the center back neck of the collar.

4. Mark the center back of the neckline with a pin or fabric marking tool.

5. Matching up the raw (unfolded) edge of the collar to the raw edge of the neckline, with right sides of the fabrics facing each other, pin the center mark of the collar to the center mark on the neckline. *Fig. F*

6. Pin the base of the collar panel to the bottom hem of the vest.

7. Working from the center out, pin the rest of the collar in place.

8. Sew the first side of the collar into place, using a ¼″ (6mm) seam allowance.

TIP • Easy Does It!
When sewing the collar into place, sew from the center out. This ensures that the collar will lay evenly along the neckline.

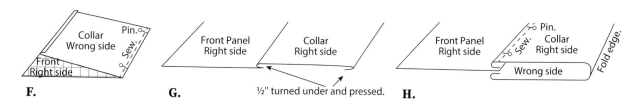

9. Press the seam toward the collar. *Fig. G*

10. Fold the collar in half lengthwise along the pressed line so the right side is facing out and the collar encases the raw seam. Overlap the raw seam by ½″ (1.2cm).

11. Pin the collar into place, being careful to pin the collar flat so as not to skew the 2 sides of the collar while sewing.

12. From the right side of the garment, topstitch ⅛″ (3mm) from the folded edge, being sure to sew through the ½″ (1.2cm) folded seam and the raw seam. *Fig. H*

> **NOTE • Use an Edge-Stitch Foot**
> We like using an edge-stitch foot for this process to keep the seam super-straight.

Bind the Bottom and Armhole Hems

1. With right sides facing each other, place opened/flat 1½″ (38mm) bias tape along the entire bottom hem seam. Be careful to not stretch the tape.

2. Sew ¼″ (6mm) seam along the entire bottom hem.

3. Fold the bias tape over the seam, finger-pressing if needed.

4. Turning to the inside of the garment, with wrong sides facing, fold the remaining raw edge of the tape to the center line and fold the tape over the fabric, encasing the raw edge.

5. Pin the tape into place.

6. From the front of the garment, stitch-in-the-ditch along the sewn tape, being sure to catch the folded edge on the inside. You can also slipstitch or whipstitch the back edge closed.

7. Using the same method, bind the raw edge around the armholes.

Final Touches

Press or steam the garment as needed and then adorn your fabulous self and go strut your stuff in the wild. And commit this phrase to heart: "Thank you, I made it!"

ABOUT US

Shannon Roudhán and Jason Bowlsby are the dynamic DIY duo from Seattle, Washington. Their award-winning crochet, knit, quilting, handwork, embroidery, and sewing designs have been featured in and on the covers of domestic and international publications, and their craft, portrait, and fashion photography has appeared in books and magazines around the globe. Shannon & Jason have published twelve books, including *Complete Crochet Course – The Ultimate Reference Guide* and *Designer Crochet*. Their latest books, *Boro & Sashiko, Harmonious Imperfection* and *Contemporary Kogin-zashi: Modern Sashiko Beyond Filling in the Gaps*, are available from C&T Publishing. You are, currently, holding lucky book number thirteen in your hands.

The duo have been married for 28 years and have been teaching adults for 20+ years. With their mastery of subjects from crochet and knitting to photography, spinning, embroidery, sewing, and quilting, their enthusiasm, quirky sense of humor, and relatable teaching style have made them sought-after teachers in virtual, local, and national venues. They also have a wide range of live and recorded online classes available from Creative Spark Online and other online platforms. The "edu-tainment" experience of a class with Shannon & Jason will leave you informed, empowered, and in stitches (see what we did there?).

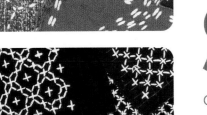

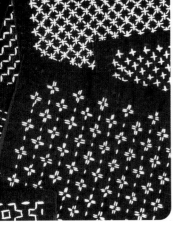

CREATIVE SPARK

ONLINE LEARNING

Embroidery courses to become an expert embroiderer...

From their studio to yours, Creative Spark instructors are teaching you how to create and become a master of your craft. So not only do you get a look inside their creative space, you also get to be a part of engaging courses that would typically be a one or multi-day workshop from the comfort of your home.

Creative Spark is not your one-size-fits-all online learning experience. We welcome you to be who you are, share, create, and belong.

Scan for a gift from us!

creativespark.ctpub.com